Practical Recording 2

Also in this series and available from **smt**:

Practical Recording 1: Microphones
Practical Recording 3: Cubase SX
Practical Recording 4: Rhythm Programming (second edition)
Practical Recording 5: Surround Sound
Practical Recording 6: Music On Mac OS X
Practical Recording 7: Reason
Practical Recording 8: Logic 6

Printed and bound in the United Kingdom by MPG Books, Bodmin

Published by SMT, an imprint of Sanctuary Publishing Limited, Sanctuary House, 45-53 Sinclair Road, London W14 0NS, United Kingdom

www.sanctuarypublishing.com

First published in Germany under the title *Pro Tools In Der Praxis*, PPVMEDIEN GmbH, 2003. Text © Mark Ziebarth and Christian Preissig, 2003

Cover photograph courtesy of Keith Williams @ sprout.uk.com ltd. All other images courtesy of the authors and Johannes Maul, Digidesign, a division of Avid Technology GmbH

ISBN: 1-84492-056-9

Practical Recording 2

Pro Tools

Christian Preissig and Mark Ziebarth

smt

CONTENTS

ON THE CD

Whilst we have set out in this book to explain how Pro Tools works including all the underlying ideas, nothing beats learning by doing. For this reason, a CD is included with the book, containing the following:

- Demo versions of plug-ins
- Pro Tools demo session
- Original documentation in the form of Read Me files and PDFs
- The application itself in the form of a hardware-independent version of Pro Tools Free for Macintosh and PC

Pro Tools Free is the ideal way to get started using Pro Tools, since all the operations relating to recording, editing and mixing are identical with those of the TDM version. The principal constraint relates to the number of available tracks, which are limited to eight audio and 48 MIDI tracks. Naturally Pro Tools Free does not support TDM plug-ins as the requisite hardware is missing. Native plug-in formats such as AudioSuite and RTAS can be loaded, which is why you will find in the Plug-in Demos folder, installation programs for a large number of Digidesign plug-ins for whichever operating system you happened to use. Try them out in your sessions or on the demo song 'Be There LE' which is included.

Practice Beats Study

Naturally the Pro Tools demo session included on the disk provides you with an excellent opportunity to try out the various edit and arrange functions of Pro Tools. Cut, paste, move and automate the data of the session to your heart's content or create your own mix – with what you've learned already, it should be a breeze. And in the event that you still do not understand something, try consulting the original manuals dealing with Pro Tools Free, the plug-ins and the OMS as well as Digidesign's own software reference manual. You will find them all in the Release Notes and Documentation folder.

ABOUT THIS BOOK

Practical Recording 2: Pro Tools describes the system and the various techniques involved in operating it, through the use of typical studio situations. It examines Pro Tools, what it is capable of and how it works, and provides a host of practical tips, as well as supplying the background knowledge needed to work intuitively with the system and well.

Taking the form of an introduction and written in clear, simple language, *Practical Recording 2: Pro Tools* draws upon the authors' vast studio experience to provide a wealth of information and practical suggestions you can use immediately in your own working environment.

The book is aimed at ambitious hobby musicians, students of sound engineering, people who work in advertising agencies, studios, TV production, trainees – in short, everyone who uses or intends to use Pro Tools.

ABOUT THE AUTHORS

Christian Preissig was born in 1967 and is a qualified audio engineer, managing the production firm Media dell' Arte – Text & Ton in Erlangen. As well as working as an editor for the German music magazine *KEYS*, he is a consultant in Documentation/Localisation to numerous companies in the pro audio/video sector, being responsible at the same time for their audio planning. His main field of activity is music production in the rock and pop genres and the addition of sound to multimedia projects for industry. Since 1996, he has relied exclusively on Digidesign hardware, having begun with Session 8 and switched to Pro Tools TDM systems in 1998.

Mark Ziebarth was born in 1967 in Oldenburg. After graduating from high school and completing his military service, he studied in Hamburg, then worked for the Public Prosecutor's Office in Hamburg before becoming an editor of *KEYS* magazine in 1998. In the same year, he returned to Hamburg, where he has worked ever since as a composer and music producer. With his own Pro Tools system, Ziebarth has produced TV advertisements for Toyota, Seat, Deutsche Post, Wella, Mercedes Benz and Hornbach among others as well as cinema advertisements for Lucky Strike, West and others. During all this time, he has continued to contribute regularly to *KEYS*.

INTRODUCTION: MUSIC AND SOUND TODAY

Today's music projects and post-production sessions are created with the computer – in professional environments almost exclusively using Pro Tools. In this introduction, we would like to explain a number of key concepts and procedures that will make the rest of the book easier to understand. Armed with this basic knowledge, you should be able to master the rest of the book without difficulty.

Modern Production

Analogue recording and mixing were yesterday; a state-of-the-art computer and Pro Tools hard- and software are today. Modern productions are supported largely by the twin pillars of hard disk recording and the musical instruments digital interface (MIDI) and have little in common with the stereotype people have in their heads of a room full of equipment, with the reels of tape machines turning silently in the background. Nowadays virtually all productions are exclusively digital; tape recorders are only used in a few exceptional situations.

Digital Production

Without going into the finer details of the digitisation of audio signals, you need to understand certain basic concepts relating to the process and its results. To digitise an audio signal, you need an analogue-to-digital (A/D) converter, which converts the waveform of a microphone, for example, into a format a computer can work with: binary numbers, that is to say numbers composed entirely of ones and noughts. Two factors play an important role in this process: the sampling rate and the resolution. The sampling rate (also called the sampling frequency) is the number of snapshots of the waveform the converter takes each second – in other words, the number of times the voltage of the signal is measured. The resolution (also called the word length or bit rate) is the number of discrete values to which the measurement can be mapped and therefore determines the precision with which the state of the waveform at the time each snapshot is taken can be described.

Sampling Rates

One of the most commonly used sampling rates is 44.1kHz (since this is the standard for audio CDs), but 48kHz is nowadays the norm for television, and some of the new mediums, such as DVD Audio or Super Audio CD, employ even higher sampling frequencies such as 96kHz and even 192kHz.

Audio Resolution

The number of bits (ones or zeros) available to describe the momentary state of the waveform when each snapshot (called a sample) is taken has implications no less important to the fidelity of the audio. Audio CDs operate in 16-bit resolution but this bit rate is now seldom used during the production phase, 24-bit resolution being far commoner and with good reason: the dynamic range available when you are working in 24-bit resolution is far higher. In 16-bit resolution, you can use any of 65,000 different values to describe the state of the waveform. In 24-bit resolution, the number of available values is well over 16 million. This means it is possible to paint a far more detailed portrait of the amplitude of the signal at each point in time without turning up the level of the signal and risking distortion. Whereas the analogue distortion of guitar amps, tape recorders and audio valves is generally considered a pleasant effect and the devices in question often overloaded on purpose to produce it, digital distortion sounds horrible and is to be avoided at all costs.

Music Production And Post-Production

Before delving into the details of either, we should first get straight the difference between music production and post-production. The former is the process of recording, editing, mixing and mastering audio, the end result being perhaps a CD. The latter is a term derived from the world of cinema and describes everything that is done to the film or video material once the shooting is finished. Nowadays post-production is largely performed using computers.

Post-Production

A further distinction ought really to be made between audio post-production and video post-production, but since audio professionals generally work on the sound only and leave the video editing to specialists, they generally drop the word 'audio' unless there is some risk of ambiguity. By 'post-production', audio professionals mean the recording, editing, mixing and mastering of the sound that accompanies the images, whether it be dialogue, narration, sound effects, music or any combination of the four – sound design and the creation of the illusion of space being two of the most crucial disciplines in modern post-production.

An example may make all this clearer. For the production of a TV advertisement, a recording studio will be commissioned to create the audio material. Usually the end result will consist of a balanced mix of music, one or more voices, and various other types of sound. The recording studio will hire a composer to write the music, an actor (probably) to provide the voice-over and a sound designer to supply the miscellaneous sounds. When all these have finished their work, the job of the mixing engineer is to blend the various elements together in the right proportions and add the sound to the video material. Of course, when post-production begins, the music will normally already have been mixed; the mix engineer is unlikely to want to change the volume ratios of the various instruments, for example; all that will already have been done; he will simply be concerned with the relative levels of the music, speech and sound design. Sound engineers are, of course, also involved in other types of production – such as radio plays – that have nothing to do with the addition of sound to film but cannot be described as music production either, but since there are no techniques of any consequence used in the production of radio plays that are not also used in post-production, we will pass over them in the discussion that follows.

Audio Tracks, Regions And The Timeline

Pro Tools – like virtually all modern systems – is based upon hard disk recording. The audio signal is recorded to, and played back from, what is termed an audio track and stored on the hard disk in the form of an audio file. Audio tracks differ from the tracks of an analogue tape recorder in many ways, one being that there is no physical connection between the recorded signal and the audio track used to record it; you may have recorded the signal on Track One, but this need not stop you playing it back on Tracks Two, Three, Four on any other.

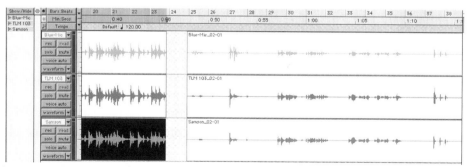

Audio tracks and regions in Pro Tools

In the Edit window, each audio track occupies a separate line of the display. Within each track, the recorded signal is displayed in the form of a coloured waveform (representing the amplitude of the signal) framed by a rectangle known as a region (or audio region to be precise). At the time the signal is recorded, a region is created that has the same duration (represented by its horizontal extent) as the recording. In fact though, the region consists of nothing more than playback parameters that refer to the audio file on the hard disk. You can therefore shorten, cut, move, copy and do all kinds of other things to the region without the underlying reality, the audio file itself, being altered in any way. This is one of the great beauties of hard-disk recording and is known as non-destructive editing. The significance is that the length, and position along the time axis, of a region can be altered at will, and you can even create multiple regions, all of which refer to the same audio file, without once having to copy the actual audio data that is on the disk.

Regions are arranged on screen along a horizontal time axis, the scale of which can be increased or decreased at will. When working with music, it is normal for the time axis to be divided into bars and beats. When adding sound to film, on the other hand, the orientation is usually provided by a time code calibrated in hours, minutes and images per second. In either case, the time axis in Pro Tools is known as the timeline.

And there we have the essential structure of the display. The tracks are arranged one on top the other like lines of text on a page. Within each track, the individual regions (if there is more than one and assuming that they do not overlap) are arranged from left to right along the horizontal timeline in the order in which they sound., whilst a grid, displayed in the background like the lines on a piece of graph paper, is used to indicate the distribution of bars and beats along the timeline.

MIDI

In addition to audio tracks, modern music productions are liable to contain multiple MIDI tracks. These consist not of audio material but of MIDI messages that are used to control tone generators such as synthesisers and samplers. To take the case of a synth track, what is stored at the time of recording is not the actual sound of the synthesiser but a set of messages that describe the actions of the performer – that he struck a particular key, for example, at a particular time, with a particular degree of force. When the MIDI track is played back, these messages are interpreted by the synthesiser as commands ('act as though a performer had struck that particular key, at that particular time, with that degree of force') and in this way the original performance is recreated. Of course, if no tone generator is connected at the time the track is played back, you will hear nothing at all.

So the Edit window displays a multi-layer sandwich of audio and MIDI tracks. The tracks are arranged initially in order of seniority, with the first to be created – regardless of whether it is an audio or a MIDI track – on top.

Sequencers

A device intimately connected with the concept of MIDI is what is known as a sequencer. Even though Pro Tools differs in many respects from the classic sequencer applications such as Cubase or Logic, there is no denying a certain similarity. A sequencer is an application (in other words, a computer program) that records and plays back MIDI messages. When they were first introduced, Cubase and Logic had no audio functions – these were only added later – so they were called MIDI sequencers. Later, when audio tracks were added, people began to call them audio sequencers, though of course they were now both, since all the functions relating to MIDI were retained. With Pro Tools, the development was the other way about. In the first version of the program, there were only audio tracks. It is the MIDI functionality that was added later.

Quantization

Another word intimately bound up with MIDI and MIDI sequencers in the field of audio production is quantization. Quantization is a way of forcing a MIDI note that falls between two particular lines in the timeline grid to move (or snap) automatically to (or closer to) one of the lines on either side of it – usually the nearest. It is up to you to determine the mesh of the grid, that is to say, whether the note in question should snap to the nearest minim, crotchet, quaver or whatever (US: half note, quarter note, eight note and so on). Quantization provides a quick and painless way of ironing out timing irregularities in a performance. If you are playing a passage of semiquavers (US 16th notes) and you make a less than perfect job of it, all you need to do is set the mesh of the grid to 'semiquavers', quantize, and all the notes that fell between the lines of the grid, because they were slightly mistimed, will move magically to the nearest line so that it will sound as though you played the passage with perfect metric regularity. The problem, of course, is that this is sometimes taking matters altogether too far. You don't want the performance to sound mechanical and for this reason more sophisticated quantization options are available for professional recording, one such being 'grooves', which can be thought of as user-defined quantization patterns.

Computers, Processing Power And Hard Disks

To work with Pro Tools, you obviously need a computer. Digidesign supports both Windows and the Mac OS. Even if nowadays virtually every computer produced satisfies the minimum requirements in terms of processing speed and the provision of interfaces, it is advisable when choosing a computer to select one of the configurations recommended by Digidesign with a view to achieving optimal performance and the requisite degree of stability; it will also ensure that you receive technical support in case of need. What all Pro Tools systems have in common is that they complement your computer through the addition of audio hardware consisting mainly of one or more PCI cards that are slotted into the motherboard of your computer and one or more external interfaces that are used for making audio connections and usually also contain the converters.

Hard disk recording makes far greater demands upon the processing power of your computer than applications such as word processors, since during recording and playback, vast amounts of data have to be written to and read from the hard disk in real time, and this alone involves massive overheads. Another problem is that the free space on your hard disk may run low unless you transfer finished projects to some other medium for archiving. As a rule of thumb, a single audio track in 24-bit resolution with a sampling rate of 44.1kHz will consume 7.5MB of hard disk space per minute. Make that 24 tracks and it comes to 180MB per minute. Make it 32 tracks and it's 240MB per minute. On the plus side, if you use the same signal in two or more sessions – in multiple versions of the same song, for example – Pro Tools will access the same audio file for all sessions and not waste hard disk space by copying it. In such cases, doubling the number of sessions does not involve doubling your storage requirements.

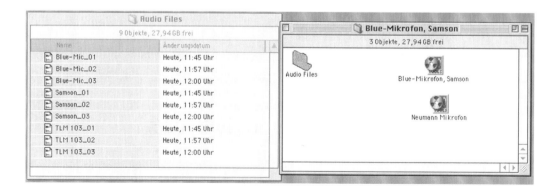

Both sessions are accessing the same audio files, so you can create an alternative version of your session without consuming much additional disk space

Mixing, Software Mixers And Plug-ins

Pro Tools not only replaces the multi-track recorder, it replaces the classical mixing console as well, because the work in the recording studio is seldom over when the last signal has been recorded. Indeed much of the art of music production lies in the mixing. The job of mixing, in the simplest case, consists of getting the balance between two or more signals right. To assist in this endeavour, Pro Tools provides a software mixer the interface of which includes an onscreen representation of a mixing console. In this onscreen mixer, a separate channel strip is assigned to each audio or MIDI track.

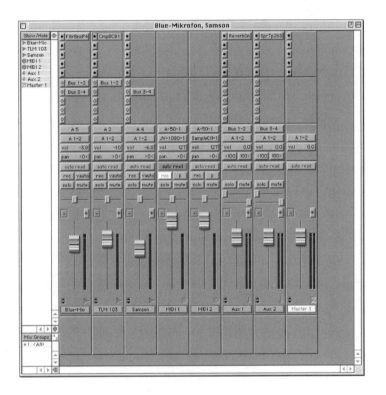

The art is in the mixing – Pro Tools software mixer offers all the functionality of a high-end mixing console

Effects

Nowadays, of course, the job of mixing involves far more than simply regulating volume levels, one key task being the addition of effects such as reverberation, compression and EQ, and another, the creation of a stereo or surround image from the recorded material. Effects processing within Pro Tools is provided for the most part by what are called plug-ins, these being routines (that is to say, program fragments) loaded into the main program on an ad hoc basis to perform particular tasks. The tasks in question generally involve a great deal of processing, and if excessive use is made of them, the overheads can be considerable.

Software tone generators are integrated into the main program in much the same way as effects plug-ins. They come in the shape of synthesisers or samplers the processing of which is done within Pro Tools rather than by the processors or some external hardware device. The range of available software instruments is growing fast and offers exciting possibilities for expanding your Pro Tools system. Of course it must again be borne in mind that software tone generators also impose a considerable drain on the processing power of your system.

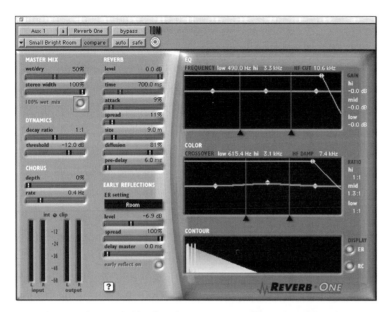

Reverb One from Digidesign is an outstanding TDM plug-in

An outstanding software synthesiser: the Virus TDM is just as good as the hardware original

Processing Power

The power of your Pro Tools system depends upon various factors, primary among them being the version of Pro Tools with which you are working. The Free version, which you will find on the CD that accompanies this book, provides a maximum of eight audio tracks, even though your computer may be powerful enough to handle far more. Pro Tools LE, on the other hand, is capable of recording and playing

back up to 32, and Pro Tools TDM (HD) up to 128, audio tracks at once.

If you are using plug-ins, you will need an even more powerful system. Different Pro Tools systems employ different strategies for satisfying the demand for processing power. Both Pro Tools Free and also Pro Tools LE are host-based, meaning that they rely upon the central processing unit (CPU) of your computer to handle the audio tracks, plug-ins and software tone generators. Pro Tools TDM systems, on the other hand, come with processors of their own (known as digital signal processors or DSPs) that have been specially designed for audio processing and are located on the TDM cards that slot into your motherboard. Each such card contains several DSPs and one of the considerable advantages of TDM systems is that you can upgrade your system by adding additional cards. In that way, you can achieve effortlessly a degree of processing power far superior to that of host-based systems.

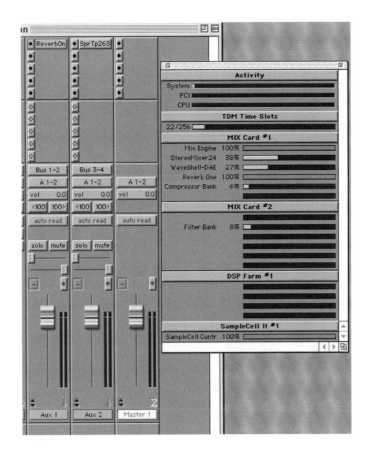

With TDM systems, a special window indicates how many DSPs are currently being used by plug-ins

1 SYSTEM CONFIGURATION

Host Or TDM?

Pro Tools systems can be divided into two basic categories: host-based and TDM. All systems delivered with the software Pro Tools LE are host-based and therefore use the CPU of your computer to run the plug-ins. Software bearing the name Pro Tools without the suffix LE is designed for the large TDM systems and offers additional functions, such as special synchronisation capabilities or the integration of special hardware like that needed to integrate high-resolution video into a Pro Tools session. The application Pro Tools Free, which you will find on the CD accompanying this book and can also download from the Digidesign web site, www.digidesign.com, is also host-based, but offers far fewer possibilities than Pro Tools LE: you cannot, for example, use more than eight audio tracks, even though your computer may have the power to process a far greater number. However as a learning aid, and to provide a foretaste of the possibilities offered by Pro Tools, this version is ideal.

TDM Systems

TDM systems are Digidesign's top-of-the-line products, though here, too, there are differences, since a great deal has changed since the first TDM buss systems were introduced in 1993 and 1994. Pro Tools|HD is the latest product line and features the most powerful systems currently available. Pro Tools|24 MIX is, so to speak, the predecessor series, though it has not been withdrawn from the market, whilst Pro Tools 24 and Pro Tools III must now be considered obsolete hardware. With Pro Tools|HD, the TDM buss has been redesigned, so it is incompatible with the old audio interfaces and

DSP cards. Pro Tools TDM systems are essentially modular in structure to allow users to assemble systems tailor-made to their own needs and invariably include both DSP cards and audio interfaces. TDM systems are also expandable in a variety of directions and employ the full version of the Pro Tools software.

Hardware

The power of the various TDM systems varies enormously, depending upon the power of the DSP cards and audio interfaces with which they are equipped.

Pro Tools|HD

The flagship of the Pro Tools series offers up to 128 audio tracks, although the track count is reduced when working with high definition audio at 96 or 192kHz. Needless to say, the system operates in 24-bit resolution. Compared with its predecessor, Pro Tools MIX, not only have the digital signal processors on the DSP cards been improved but also the audio interfaces. An HD card offers nine identically equipped and very powerful DSPs, and an HD system can consist of up to seven such cards, thereby guaranteeing vast reserves of processing power. The audio interfaces employed by Pro Tools|HD comprise the top-of-the-line 192 I/O and the smaller 96 I/O (max 96kHz), each of which offers, in addition to outstanding A/D- and D/A-converters, a wide variety of digital interfaces and synchronisation options.

When purchasing an HD system, you have three basic configurations to choose from: HD 1, HD 2 and HD 3. The top system, HD 3, comes with three HD cards and can be combined with either of the above-mentioned audio interfaces. The HD 2 comes with two

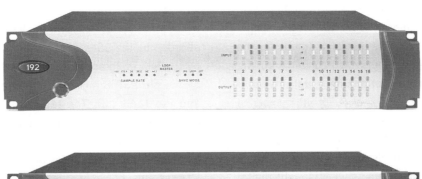

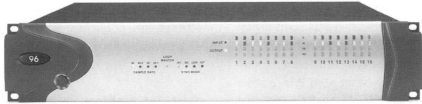

HD systems employ state-of-the-art audio interfaces

cards and the HD 1, a single card. If you think you might be needing more cards somewhere along the line, it makes sense to invest in a larger system in the first place, as purchasing additional HD processing cards at a later date is likely to work out considerably more expensive.

Pro Tools|24 MIX

With the introduction of the HD systems, the MIX

systems now find themselves in the second row. MIX cards comprise six DSPs that are somewhat less powerful than those offered by the HD cards. Their maximum sampling rate is 48kHz and no more than 64 audio tracks can be heard simultaneously. Twenty-four-bit recording is possible, provided you choose an audio interface that offers this resolution. MIX systems also come with up to seven DSP cards, and here, too, there is a choice of audio interfaces including the

The audio interfaces for MIX systems offer a wide variety of options for analogue and digital connection

888|24, the 882|20, the 1622 I/O and the ADAT Bridge. The interfaces beginning with an '8' follow a simple numbering convention: the first digit stands for the number of analogue inputs (A/D-converters), the second, for the number of analogue outputs (D/A-converters), and the third, 2 or 8, for the number of digital inputs and outputs. The number following the 'I' denotes the word length (bit resolution) of the A/D-converters. The qualitatively superior 888|24 therefore offers 24-bit A/D-converters as well as eight digital inputs and outputs in AES/EBU format. The 1622 I/O offers 16 A/D-converters operating in 20-bit resolution and two D/A-converters, whilst the ADAT Bridge offers *inter alia* 16 channels equipped with ADAT optical digital connectors (16 inputs and 16 outputs).

Pro Tools|24 And Pro Tools III

These two systems are now long outdated. They still use the old DSP Farms, which offered only four DSPs per card. The DSPs in question are also far less powerful than those of a MIX Farm, let alone those of an HD card. It must be possible to acquire the older Pro Tools III, which does offer TDM (though only 16 tracks) for a reasonable price nowadays on the second-hand market. With Pro Tools|24, 32 audio tracks and 24-bit resolution are possible. Both these systems, however, use the old DSPs, which are no longer supported by modern TDM plug-ins. The appropriate audio interfaces are the 888 and 882, both of which perform their A/D-conversion in 18-bit resolution, and these, too, can be purchased quite cheaply on the second-hand market.

TDM Specification

The designation TDM, which stands for Time Division Multiplexing, denotes more than just highly professional audio hardware. TDM is a complex buss system for the processing of audio data.

Understanding TDM

To make the best use of a TDM system, you need first to make an informed assessment of its processing power, and the key to any such assessment lies in understanding the nature and function of both the DSPs and the timeslots. The number and type of DSPs

with which a TDM system is equipped is largely determinative of its power. Maximum power is afforded by the DSPs of the new HD cards, followed by the MIX DSPs and the so-called Merle DSPs used by the old DSP Farms (for the systems Pro Tools III and Pro Tools 24). The total processing power is obviously a function of the number of DSPs as well as their power; whilst the DSP Farms offer only four, MIX cards offer seven DSPs, and HD cards nine. With MIX systems, however, it is possible to integrate old DSP Farms, whereas Pro Tools|HD is compatible with neither MIX cards nor DSP Farms.

Timeslot Problem

With all systems other than Pro Tools|HD, the number of available timeslots can impose limitations, since both MIX systems and all previous systems are based on the old TDM Buss I, which offered only 256. Timeslots are data pathways used every time the TDM buss is accessed; every connection in the TDM mixer – whether it be a plug-in insert, a send or any other routing assignment – requires a timeslot. With larger systems, involving three, four or even more cards, it is possible to run out of timeslots, which means that even though you may have spare DSPs available, you cannot access them. To remedy this problem, the TDM Buss II employed by Pro Tools|HD features a totally new architecture that not only offers a greater number of timeslots (512 at 48kHz) but also makes more efficient use of them, since, except in the case where a connection has to be made between the first and last DSPs in the line, each timeslot can be used more than once.

Processing Power

The modern TDM systems, MIX and HD, differ from earlier systems in being able to make use of the processing power of the host computer (Pro Tools software Versions 5.1 and better) as well as that of the DSPs on the cards. Many plug-ins offer users the choice of employing a DSP or the CPU of the host computer to handle their processing needs. With the increasing processing power of modern computers, well-considered use of the host CPU can considerably enhance the overall performance of the system.

Pro Tools: The Software

The Pro Tools software is of the highest quality and satisfies fully the requirements of professional use. Particularly notable is the outstanding automation, which with its very high resolution is of the highest quality. With modern TDM systems, like MIX and HD, the Pro Tools software offers 64 busses, making it possible to master even the most exacting surround tasks. And since it allows you to define main- and sub-paths, the creation of complex film mixes with separate sums for dialogue, music and sound effects, poses no problem.

LE Systems

The LE systems are designed for smaller scale applications. They are called LE systems because they are delivered with the Pro Tools LE software, though their hardware, too, differs in many respects from that of the larger systems.

The Limitations Of Pro Tools LE

Certain system parameters are the same for all LE hardware configurations, as they reflect limitations imposed by the LE version of the Pro Tools software. For example, no LE systems will play back more than 32 audio tracks simultaneously, even if your computer is capable of processing a larger number. An LE setup has only 16 busses available for effects sends and returns and the like. For larger projects, you are expected to use a TDM system.

Digi 002

The top product among Digidesign's host-based systems is not just an audio system but also a fully-functional eight-channel mixing controller. It can even be used as an independent digital mixer, with dynamics, EQ, reverb and delay, even when no computer is connected. The FireWire interface is used to link the computer to the Digi 002, so laptops and other computers with PCI slots can also benefit from this system; an audio hard disk can be connected to the second FireWire port. Digi 002 combines with a computer and an additional hard disk to create a fully-functional small studio, complete with a headphone output, MIDI connections and microphone preamps. Digi 002 offers eight analogue inputs and outputs, four microphone preamps with phantom power,

Digi 002: top-of-the-line hardware for Pro Tools LE

digital ports, eight touch-sensitive faders and plenty else besides.

Digi 001

This system offers eight analogue inputs and outputs and up to ten digital I/Os. It is also equipped with a MIDI interface, two integrated microphone preamps with phantom power, a headphone output and a separate monitor output – it constitutes, in other words, a reliable package for small studio applications as well as ambitious home recording.

Mbox

Unlike most of the other Digidesign systems, the Mbox does not come in the form of a PCI card with an audio interface but as a USB audio interface. This means that the Mbox is also suitable for computers like Notebooks and iMacs that have no PCI slots. It is equipped with two analogue and digital inputs and

The Digi 001 offers all you need for your project studio: analogue and digital inputs and outputs, microphone preamps and MIDI

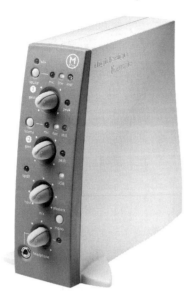

Digidesign's Mbox – ideal for the mobile studio

outputs, two Focusrite microphone preamps with phantom power, a headphone output and a Zero Latency Monitoring function, designed primarily to allow instrumentalists or singers when recording to hear their own signal without having to endure the distracting delays unavoidable with host-based systems. Thanks to its compactness, the Mbox is especially suitable for mobile use.

Audiomedia III
Of all the available Pro Tools systems, Audiomedia III is the oldest, and the design is a little outdated. Nowadays, two analogue and digital inputs and outputs on a PCI card with no other extras does not add up to an especially tempting package. However, anyone who does still possess an Audiomedia III system or succeeds in acquiring one cheaply on the

second hand market will nonetheless be able to run a Pro Tools LE system with it.

Processing Power
Unlike with TDM systems, the power of an LE system depends entirely upon the speed of the computer. Plug-ins involve particularly high processing overheads; without even needing to consult the Show System Usage window, you can tell often from its sluggish handling of the graphics that the computer is running out of steam.

Problem Areas
Despite the blistering pace of development in recent years in the area of computer-assisted music production, a number of problems have yet to be fully resolved.

Live Inputs
We speak of a 'live input' when, for example, a synthesiser signal is looped through the audio system in the computer and fed into the mix via a software mixer. The result is a slight delay (known as *latency*) that has two causes: the intrinsic delay that results from looping the signal through the audio system and the processing performed by plug-ins. With Pro Tools TDM systems, the delay is kept to an absolute minimum – a few samples, no more – so live inputs pose no problems, but with host-based systems, whilst it is nowadays possible to reduce latency to well under ten milliseconds, doing so imposes a considerable drain on the power of the audio system. With host-based systems, in other words, you have to choose between short delays and fewer plug-ins or more plug-ins and longer delays. It is advisable, therefore, to make only sparing use of live inputs with host-based systems. If you intend to use them extensively, you would be far better off with a TDM system.

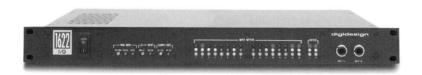

The 1622 I/O audio interface was specially designed for the integration of live inputs into TDM systems

Studio Cables

With so much of the work of the studio confined to the computer, there is far less cable to worry about nowadays, but it is still important to use balanced connections wherever possible. Balanced leads are impervious to interference and can therefore carry the audio signal over far greater distances without loss of quality. Over very short distances, it may be permissible to use unbalanced connections in exceptional circumstances, but apart from the individual outputs 3–8 on the Digi 001, all analogue inputs and outputs of Pro Tools systems are equipped for balanced operation. S/PDIF digital connections on RCA jacks are also unbalanced. They, too, should therefore be reserved for short distances.

Level

As well as using balanced connections, it is important even with analogue signals to pay attention to the level. In studios, the standard is +4dBu, but many devices designed for home use operate at −10dBV. As a rule, therefore, Pro Tools interfaces allow you to switch between these two levels. In principle, it makes no real difference which you use, as long as you do not mix the two, as the unnecessary amplification that results is prejudicial to signal quality.

Care must also be taken that the level of the signal fed to the A/D-converters is sufficiently high, if you want to make the best use of the system's dynamic range. If you only record 16-bit files to your hard disk, you need to be especially punctilious in this respect. On the other hand, digital distortion must be avoided, too, as it can ruin any recording. When you're working in 24-bit, you can afford to be more relaxed and use lower levels that leave plenty of headroom for signal peaks.

Pro Tools 6: The Next Generation

While the tried-and-tested series 5 systems are anything but obsolete, Pro Tools 6 is now state of the art. But rest assured: in terms of work flow, next to nothing has changed; the new version is just as easy to work with as its predecessor. That isn't to say the changes are purely cosmetic. Far from it. The look of the program *has* improved dramatically, but new functions have also been added, and under the bonnet things a revolution has taken place.

Cross-Platform And LE Enhancements

The old core of the program has been discarded and a new engine better adapted to the demands of modern operating systems such as the Mac OS X and Windows

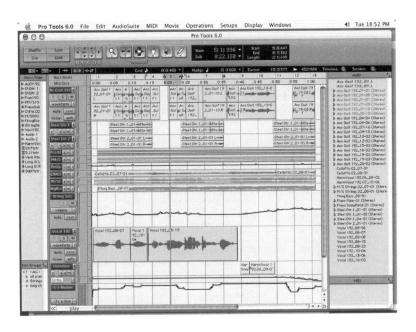

The new Pro Tools 6, engineered for Mac OS X

XP inserted in its place. On the Windows platform, the improvements in stability and performance are particularly marked, and whilst Windows has so far played only a minor role in the TDM market, in view of the proliferation of LE systems on the PC the improvements are long overdue. Unfortunately the launch of Pro Tools 6 for Windows was delayed several months, so Windows users had to wait for Version 6.1 to make the switch.

There is also good news for users of Pro Tools LE, as several TDM features are now also offered by the LE software. These include single key shortcuts, the highly useful Time Compression/Expansion (TC/E) trim tool, which allows you to trim the length of an audio region to match that of another region, a tempo template, a video scene or other reference, and the Inactive Tracks function.

Support For Mac OS X

One of the most important innovations in Pro Tools 6 is support for Apple's latest operating system, Mac OS X (OS 9 is no longer supported). The result is considerably enhanced performance and the long awaited support for multi-processor computers. Pro Tools is now capable of passing the operating system several threads that it can process independently, so moving the transport window, for example, no longer interferes with the display of the level meter.

Another improvement is the new multi-user login functionality, which enables individual users to save their own custom display, operation, editing, automation, processing, compatibility and MIDI preferences – a feature that will be greatly appreciated by operators who share a workstation.

With the switch to Mac OS X, the look of Pro Tools has also changed. Not only are the mix, edit and transport windows now more attractively presented but their functionality has also been enhanced. The layout of the Mix window in narrow mode is far clearer. Discreet use has been made of colour, with functionality rather than aesthetics in mind. Fortunately Digidesign has resisted the temptation to indulge in cloying, brightly coloured images that only serve in the course of a long session to get on your nerves. Theoretically, Pro Tools is now also 'localisable', which means it should be able to communicate with the user in German, French or even Japanese if the need should arise, though it is not yet clear how much, if any, use Digidesign intends to make of this possibility.

Improved Organisation

Data management has long been an area woefully neglected by all designers of hard-disk recording systems. With DigiBase and the optional DigiBase Pro, Pro Tools 6 has taken an important step forward.

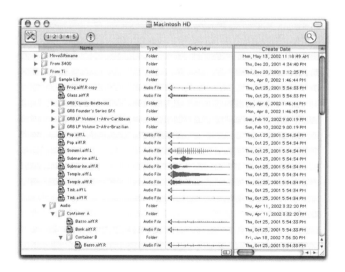

An important step forward in the area of data management: the new Volume Browser

The point is that it's often difficult – especially with large sessions – to keep track of where all the elements of the session have been stored. Audio and video data are often stored on different hard disks, and when you are working simultaneously on several projects at once and using several different storage mediums (external hard disks, effects CDs and the like) at the same time, the possibility of confusion increases exponentially.

Essentially, DigiBase is similar in operation to the Finder on the Macintosh or Windows Explorer and serves to help you manage the system's files. DigiBase gives you access to all the important information about a file, including its length, timestamp and two user comment fields. To simplify the search still further, you can customise the layout of this information, so that only the criteria that most interests you is displayed and the rest ignored.

The Task Manager

Before importing a file into Pro Tools, you can view a thumbnail of the waveform and audition the file (beginning wherever you like) – regardless of the sample rate or data format being used in the session. As soon as you drag and drop the file onto the timeline, the file is automatically copied to the session folder and, if need be, converted to the correct format. The copying and conversion as well as the creation of fades are processed in the background in Pro Tools 6, so you can continue recording or editing your session whilst the Task Manager organises the whole operation. If you like, you can follow the progress of the current operation.

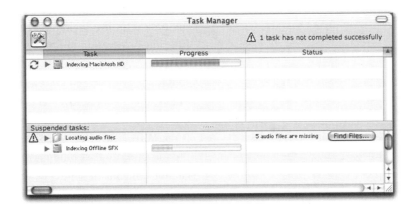

Now the conversion and copying of audio files is processed in the background thanks to the new Task Manager

The DigiBase Pro option, which is only available for TDM systems, offers a number of more far-reaching data-management possibilities including the creation and sharing of custom catalogues that can reference files stored on networks or offline media. You can also view, search and spot files from sound effects libraries or loop CDs and enter various parameters of search criteria such as file type, comment or creation date.

MIDI And The Beat Detective

Pro Tools' MIDI functions have also been improved in Version 6. The Core MIDI services have replaced the obsolete OMS as a component of the Mac OS X. The MIDI Time Stamping (MTS) that comes with this package ensures the sample-accurate transfer of MIDI data between Pro Tools and compatible software synthesisers and samplers. The timing of external MIDI devices is also handled now with far greater precision;

provided MIDI I/O or a similar MTS-compatible interface is used, it should be possible to achieve values of a millisecond or better.

Groove Quantize

Among the features of the new MIDI implementation is the extensive manipulation of rhythmic content through powerful groove creation and modification tools. The Groove Quantize feature incorporates intelligent bar/beat adjustment as well as support for the new 960ppq DigiGroove templates.

The new Groove Quantize function allows you to import new patterns

The Beat Detective

The very popular Beat Detective has also been enhanced, though unfortunately this feature remains the prerogative of TDM systems. Now it is possible to extract and generate DigiGroove templates from an audio performance, whereby both the timing and the dynamics of the extract can be applied to other

passages in the session. These new Groove Templates are fully compatible with the new Groove Injection Templates supplied by Numerical Sound.

The functions of the Beat Detective have also been extended

Non-Destructive MIDI

The new Flatten Performance function even offers the user what is in effect non-destructive MIDI, by making it possible to return a MIDI region at any time to a defined starting state, even though countless quantization steps or other edits may have been performed on the region in the meantime. The Undo function is therefore redundant.

Click

Among the other improvements in the MIDI department are an increase in the number of MIDI tracks and DirectMIDI, which enables automatic tempo broadcasting so that plug-ins such as rhythmic delays cannot drift out of sync. Pro Tools also now features an integrated Click plug-in that saves users the chore of having to wire up and program an external sound module just to generate a MIDI click.

Simple but effective – the new Click plug-in

Improved Mixing Functionality
Sharing Track Attributes

The mixing section of Pro Tools 6 also features some sensible improvements, the most obvious being the ability to transfer all track attributes from one session to another. This allows you to import any combination of audio or MIDI playlists, mixer automation, routings, plug-in instances or settings and plug-in automation. You can also choose to replace or overlay the existing data of your session. This new function should prove useful in a wide range of different situations. For example, if you have perfected a drum track in one session, you can transfer some or all of the track attributes to another session in which the drum tracks have not yet been edited. And just like changing tapes on an analogue reel-to-reel, Pro Tools 6 allows you to import MIDI and/or audio playlists without changing the mixer, routing or plug-in settings.

Defining Track Height

Another interesting feature is the ability to define a zoom for toggling track heights, such that when a region is selected, the selection always looms large in the centre of the screen.

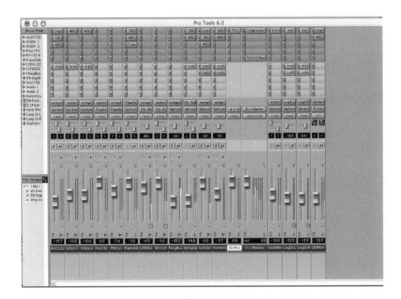

More clearly laid out and tastefully modernised – the new Mix window

Remote Control And System Requirements
Sony Nine-Pin

The workflow has also been streamlined – especially in post-production – by means of the new Machine Profile utility that enables you to create deck configuration profiles for controlling any Sony nine-pin controllable deck; there is even support for custom track name entry in each deck profile, thus removing one possible source of confusion when record-enabling tracks assigned to remote-controlled devices. The Set Time code Position function allows you to select a location in your timeline and re-enter its time code position, relatively resetting the entire timeline.

Compatibility

Aside from the need to use a modern operating system such as Mac OS X or Windows XP, the system requirements for running Pro Tools 6 are not especially high. Among the TDM systems, only Pro Tools III is not supported. Digidesign-approved Pro Tools|24, Pro Tools|24 MIX and Pro Tools|HD systems can all benefit from the new software. Among the LE systems, only Toolbox and Digi 001 are currently supported, but support for Digi 002 and Mbox will follow shortly. Windows XP support for the new features in Pro Tools 6 and OS X compatibility with AV Option|XL, Unity and MediaManager have been available since Version 6.1.

2 THE BASICS

First Steps

Whether you are using Pro Tools for music production, film soundtracks or sound design, you are likely to be working with a large number of different files and file formats that will need to be managed efficiently from within the program, edited and eventually mixed, and naturally you are going to want to be able to move swiftly from one title or sequence to the next without having to set up your system from scratch each time. Pro Tools solves these problems by keeping all the data related to a given project in a single folder, the Session Folder. Each Session Folder contains a number of sub-folders containing audio and video data, fade information and plug-in sessions as well as a Session File in which the essential structure of your project, such as the number of tracks, is stored along with mixing and configuration data.

Sessions

The first step when beginning a new project with Pro Tools is therefore the creation of a new session. Start Pro Tools and choose New Session from the File menu.

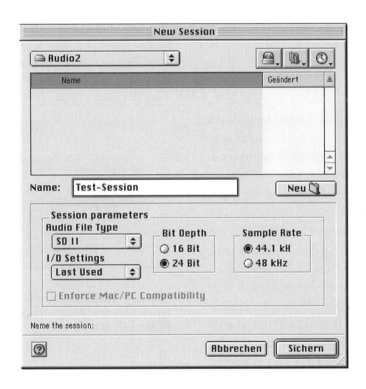

The New Session dialog, in which the session is named and the resolution defined

Beginning A New Session

In the New Session dialog box, you will enter a name, path (ie storage location) and basic settings (known as *session parameters*) for your new session.

Session Parameters

Among the first decisions you are invited to take is the file format for your audio data. The Audio File Type pop-up menu offers the choice between SDII, AIFF and WAV, the latter having been the default since Pro Tools 5.3.1. If you might want to share data across platforms with other Pro Tools users, you should also check the Enforce Mac/PC Compatibility box, which ensures the integrity of data exchange between Apple Macintosh computers and PCs running under Windows.

I/O Settings

In addition, you can choose a configuration for the inputs and outputs of your hardware – click on I/O Settings and a pop-up menu will appear listing a number of presets that cover options such as conventional music production (Stereo Mix) and surround production (5.1 Film Mix). If need be, you can create your own I/O settings, which will thereafter feature among the menu options.

Resolution

Equally important are the parameters relating to audio resolution: the Bit Depth and the Sample Rate. Whilst the older TDM systems (up to Mix), LE systems and Pro Tools Free work exclusively at sampling rates of 44.1 or 48kHz, Pro Tools|HD offers sampling rates as high as 192kHz. If you are handling a normal pop production, you will not go far wrong opting for 16-bit resolution and a sampling rate of 44.1kHz. If, on the other hand, you are recording classical music or jazz, you should be aware that 24-bit resolution will provide better dynamics and a higher signal-to-noise ratio during quiet passages. Obviously there is no point in choosing 24-bit resolution if the converters of your hardware do not offer that resolution. If you are using one of the older Digidesign interfaces such as the 882 I/O or (with Pro Tools Free) the internal converters of your computer, you should opt for 16-bit resolution. It

is worth bearing in mind that a recording in 24-bit resolution will take up approximately 50% more disk space than one in 16-bit resolution.

The Main Windows: Mix And Edit
Mixer And Tape Recorder

The user interface of Pro Tools emulates the interfaces of two of the most important devices used in traditional sound production, namely the mixing console and the tape recorder. This principle offers the possibility of routing live inputs from external sound sources to the recording medium, where they can be recorded and mixed at a single workstation. Pro Tools accordingly offers two main windows, the Mix window and the Edit window, in which to record the tracks that comprise your session, edit them and finally mix them.

Laying Tracks

Once you have created your session, you need to tailor its basic architecture to the demands of the project. You begin by creating tracks. In the File menu, choose New Track. First specify the number of new tracks you wish to create and then select their type from the pop-up menu, the options being Audio Track, Aux Input, Master Fader and MIDI Track. Except in the case of a MIDI track, you need also to select a Channel Format from between Mono, Stereo, LCR, Quad, LCRS and various surround formats (5.0 to 7.1).

The New Track dialog offers a choice of four types of track: Audio Track, Aux Input, Master Fader and MIDI Track

A distinction has to be made between, on the one hand, audio and MIDI tracks, and on the other, Aux

Inputs and Master Faders. Audio and MIDI tracks are designed for the recording and playback of data. The others are purely mixing sums that serve as recipients for physical or virtual audio streams emanating from the hardware inputs or DAE busses respectively. Consequently, no recording can be performed on these kinds of tracks.

The Mix Window

The Mix window is designed to resemble a mixing console, with the tracks offering the same functionality as analogue channel strips. Here you will find all the essential mixing functions, including faders, pan controllers, aux sends and insert send/returns, the type and number of which depend on the type of track.

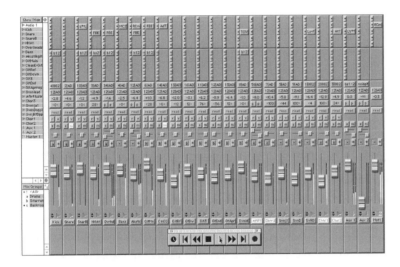

Above: Pro Tools' Mix window is modelled on the user interface of a conventional mixing console

Below: An Audio Track in the Mix window with its sections

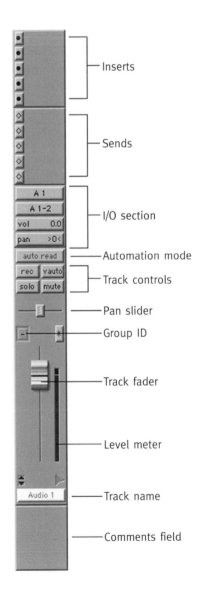

Working With The Real Time Window

The great thing about Pro Tools is that the audio and MIDI data of each track can be edited in parallel in a second window, the Edit window (see 'Edit window'). The perfect synchronicity and direct relationship between mixing parameters and audio events affords editors an extremely convenient and efficient way of working, made all the more so by the radical new possibilities afforded by automation.

The Channel Strip

The basic Pro Tools channel strip consists of the following control elements:

Inserts

The five Inserts allow you to loop plug-ins and/or the physical inputs and outputs of your hardware into the signal flow of the track. A pop-up menu is provided with the corresponding entries.

Sends

The five sends allow you to route the pre- or post-fader track signal to the virtual DAE busses and/or the physical outputs of your hardware. Again, the selection is made from a pop-up menu.

I/O Section

The two buttons at the top of the section are used for selecting the input source (DAE buses or physical inputs) and an output (DAE busses or physical outputs) via which the track signal will be emitted at the volume level determined by the Volume Fader and with the panorama settings determined by the Pan slider. Command-clicking (Mac) or Control-clicking (Windows) on the third button toggles between vol (Level), pk (Peak) and dly (Channel Delay), whereby any delay attributable to insert processing is expressed in samples.

Automation Mode

The Automation Mode Selector offers the choice between Auto-Off, -Touch, -Read, -Latch, -Write and -Trim.

Track Controls

These four software buttons serve to record-enable the track (rec), assign a voice to it (v/Voice Selector), mute the other tracks so that it can be auditioned in solo-in-place mode (solo) and mute it (mute). Command-clicking (Mac) or Ctrl-clicking (Windows) the solo button toggles on and off the Solo Safe Mode, which prevents the track being muted when you solo other tracks. This feature is especially useful for tracks such as Auxiliary Inputs as it allows you to hear an audio track together with its auxiliary effects or a MIDI track together with the software instrument assigned to it.

Pan Slider

The pan slider is used to position the track signal in the stereo image of the selected output. With mono outputs, this control is not available; in the case of multi-channel routings, it is replaced by the Multi-Format Output Window, in which you can position the signal freely in the surround field.

Group ID

The Group ID button indicates the group or groups to which the track is assigned. When you click on the button, a window appears displaying the name of each such group along with a list of its other members.

Track Fader

The track fader controls the level of the signal sent to the output or outputs to which the track is assigned.

Level Meter

The meter displays the track level. By checking and unchecking the Pre-fader Metering entry in the Operations menu, you can toggle between global pre- and post-fader metering.

Track Name

Double-clicking on the Track Name field permits you to replace the default (such as 'Audio 1' or 'MIDI 5') with a name of your own choosing (eg Lead Guitar). It is advisable to do this before you begin recording on the track, as each new file or region created on a track is auto-named after the current track name, successive takes being distinguished from one another by numbers that are tagged on the end and which increment. If you postpone renaming the track, whilst files and regions created after the change will carry the new track name, those created beforehand will still bear the (less informative) default track name.

Comments Field

When naming the track, you can also enter a comment, such as which microphone you used to record it or something similar. Thereafter this will be displayed in the Comments field beneath the track name in the channel strip.

Global Display Options

The Mix window Shows entry in the Display menu allows you to determine which information you wish to see displayed in the channel strips. By unchecking the appropriate entries, you can suppress globally (that is to say, for all channels) the display of some or all of the following sections: Comments, I/O, Inserts and Sends.

Aux Inputs

Although the layout essentially remains the same, there are minor differences between the channel strips of audio, MIDI, auxiliary input and global fader tracks. Aux inputs can be distinguished from normal audio tracks, for example, by the absence of rec and Voice Selector buttons, since you cannot record on an aux input track and it requires no voice.

Master Faders

The same is true of master fader tracks, which have no sends, pan sliders or solo and rec buttons. Input assignment is also irrelevant in this case, since master faders are only concerned with the output level of signals sent to the DAE busses or the outputs of the audio interface.

MIDI Tracks

MIDI tracks have neither inserts nor sends, since they are used for the editing not of audio signals, which are the only things effects devices can process, but of messages for the control of external tone generators or internal software instruments. In the I/O section, only MIDI devices from the current OMS setup (see Chapter 6, 'Pro Tools And MIDI') are listed and the Voice Selector parameter is replaced by a Default Program button (marked p), which determines the program change message to be sent to your instrument (so that the correct patch or sample is selected) each time the track plays.

Track Class Selection

When construction your session, you should consider at the outset, how many of each type of track you will be working with. It is a good idea to include along with the audio tracks at least one aux input and master fader, so that you can include a reverb in the monitor mix when recording. If need be, you can include one or more MIDI tracks, which will allow you to record control signals from a keyboard or drum trigger or perhaps import a pre-produced MIDI guide track. Bear in mind that for each MIDI track you can only record and playback control data for one instrument at a time. It is possible, however, to split MIDI data and distribute it to several MIDI tracks.

Reordering Tracks

If you wish to change the order in which tracks appear in the Mix window, this is easily done: just click on the track name, drag the track to the desired location and release the mouse button. This is useful as it allows you to place MIDI tracks alongside the software instruments (aux inputs) assigned to them and place instruments of the same type together.

Track Width

To conserve screen space in a large session, the Narrow Mix window option in the Display window (approximately) halves the display width not of the window but of each channel strip, so that twice as many tracks can be displayed simultaneously. Unfortunately in this case, the inevitable shortening of the track names can make orientation difficult. Another way of making more room on screen and improving the clarity of the layout is provided by the Show/Hide and Mix Groups lists on the left-side of the Mix window.

Show And Hide

The Show/Hide window lists all the tracks currently forming part of the session. Here you can decide whether or not a track should be displayed in the Mix

The Show/Hide and Mix Groups lists

window. The names of the tracks currently displayed are highlighted; hidden tracks (which remain audible) are displayed in plain text. By clicking on each name, you can toggle between showing and hiding the track. In a large session, it makes it easier sometimes to see what you are doing if you limit the display to the tracks with which you are actually working at the time.

Displaying The Essentials

In practice, you will most often want to use this function to hide auxiliary inputs and other tracks to which you do not need constant access. Naturally Pro Tools tracks the display of which has been deactivated using the Show/Hide list remain active in the signal path of your mix. It is just that you are temporarily denied access to their parameters.

Sorting The Show/Hide List

The pop-up menu at the top of the Show/Hide list offers other display options. You can for example choose to display all, only selected tracks or individual

track classes and sort the order of tracks by various criteria such as Name, Type, Mix Group, Edit Group and Voice.

Mix Groups

Other display and editing functions are available via the Mix Groups list in the lower half of the Mix window. The purpose of the list is to allow you to group tracks for editing and/or mixing. If, for example, you have recorded the same sound source using several microphones with a different track assigned to each, it is a good idea to create a separate group for these tracks so that you can mute all of them at once or control their level with a single fader. To create a group, Shift-click the names of the tracks you wish to include in the group and then select New Group from the Edit Groups pop-up menu (at the top of the list). In the dialog box that opens, enter a name for the group. Depending upon your purpose in creating it, you can either limit the group to editing (only), mixing (only) or else allow it to serve both purposes.

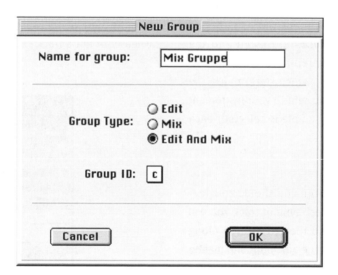

The New Group dialog allows you to name and select the type and ID of your new group

In practice, it is advisable to group for both editing and mixing the various tracks that comprise a drum take, so that you can solo the entire group together when you wish to edit problem areas. The tracks of a backing choir

on the other hand should be linked for mixing only, so that they can be edited individually but mixed together. You might wish to edit the effects track for a guitar together with the source instrument track, yet choose to mix them separately. The Mix Groups list in the Mix window only shows the groups, the tracks of which were linked using the Mix or Edit and Mix options. If you linked a group with the Edit option, the group in question will appear in the Edit Groups list in the Edit window.

Hidden Group Members

In the event that you have linked the mix functions of several tracks, you can limit them to a single channel strip in the Mix window using the Show/Hide list: alterations in the Solo, Mute or Automation status as well as the fader and aux send levels will affect hidden members of the group at the same time, so that the

relative loudness of the various tracks will remain unchanged. Whenever you wish to revert to mixing or editing the tracks singly, select Suspend All Groups from the groups list pop-up menu.

The full range of possibilities the Pro Tools interface affords for mixing are discussed in Chapter 7, 'Mixing'.

The Edit Window

Whilst the Mix window serves as a mixing console, the Edit window, in which the content of the tracks is displayed graphically as a function of time, offers a wide range of possibilities for the detailed editing of the recorded material.

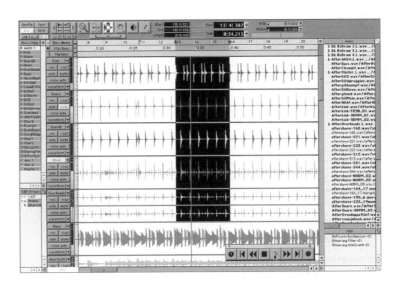

In the Edit window the tracks are stacked vertically and the horizontal access represents Time. Precise editing of the data is possible

The Edit and Mix windows share features important to both editing and mixing. The Show/Hide list, for example, is available in both windows and allows joint management of the display options. As you can see, the Mix Groups list has been replaced by an Edit Groups list. Now only those groups are displayed that were created as 'Edit' or 'Edit and Mix' groups. Otherwise the appearance and functioning of the lists is identical.

The Edit window track controls are also highly similar, and include Track Name, rec, solo, mute and voice selector buttons, to which has been added the Automation Mode selector.

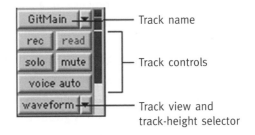

The Track Controls section provides access to key parameters

Display Options In The Edit Window

The lower two buttons, the Track View Selector and Track Height Selector, allow you to change the way the track data is displayed. The Track Height Selector varies only the height of the track, the options being Mini, Small, Medium, Large, Jumbo and Extreme, whilst the Track Display Format Selector allows you to choose the format in which the data is represented. In addition to the usual formats – Blocks, Waveforms (for audio tracks) and Notes (for MIDI tracks) – it is possible to display automation and control parameters such as volume, pan and mute status.

The Playlist

The central element in the Edit window is the Playlist Area to the right of the track controls. This is where the audio, MIDI or automation data of each track is displayed in a horizontal band, this being the currently selected *edit* or *automation playlist*. A playlist comprises one or more *regions* arranged from left to right along the time axis.

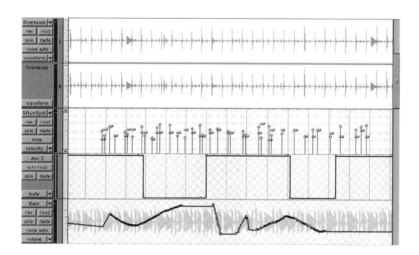

The audio, MIDI and automation data of the various tracks is displayed in the form of horizontal playlists

Playlist Contents

Depending upon its type, a track will contain either audio or MIDI and/or control data, and the content of the playlist will vary accordingly. In addition to this basic data, the playlist can be used to edit other data that relates to the mixing parameters of the track. The playlists for an audio track, for example, contain not only references (known as *regions*) to passages in the audio files, but also information about the level of the Track Fader and Pan Slider at any given instant and the status of the Mute Switch. The Track View Selector enables the display and sample-accurate editing of this data (see also the Chapters 4, 'Editing', and 7, 'Mixing').

The Playlist Is Not Linear!

In the case of audio tracks, the playlist functions as a set of instructions that tell the hard disk which parts of which audio files to read at which moment. After the first take, the playlist will likely comprise a single region (known as a Whole File region) that runs from the beginning of the track to the end and refers to a single audio file: the one you have just created. In this case, the hard disk is instructed quite simply to read the file from the beginning to the end. But as you begin editing and re-recording certain passages, the playlist will become fragmented, as the hard disk is instructed to read a little of this file, followed by a little of the next, then perhaps a second passage from the first file, then perhaps a snippet from a third, and so on. A new region begins each time the hard disk is instructed to begin reading from a new source (or recommence reading from a source the reading of which it had previously broken off); the region ends when the hard disk is instructed to cease reading from that source. In most cases, the end of one region is coincident with the start of the next, as the hard disk is told, in effect, to 'stop reading that and begin reading this'. Unlike analogue tape, which is a linear medium, the hard disk does not have to wind through an entire recording to find a passage near the end. It can jump virtually instantaneously to any part of any file at any given moment. This is called Random Access, and the upshot in the case of hard disk recording is that instead of manipulating the medium upon which the data is stored (as you had to when you wanted to splice or copying analogue tape) you can simply add or modify pointers to it. These pointers – we will call them regions from now on – can be positioned wherever and in whichever order you like, moved forwards or backwards in time, split, duplicated and edited in all manner of other ways without the underlying audio files being modified in any way.

The Audio and MIDI Regions Lists contain all the active regions in a session

Overview

Each time a new region is created, it is entered in either the Audio Regions List or the MIDI Regions List on the right hand side of the display. This is where all the regions of a session are listed, regardless of whether they represent freshly recorded material, material imported from previous sessions or are the products of editing. Entries can be dragged as needed from the region lists into the playlists where they can be repositioned at will or edited further. Any changes made to a region in a playlist are documented both there and in the region list in which it features, so edited regions remain easily identifiable for further use. Pop-up menus in the Audio and MIDI Regions Lists allow you to export regions to other applications, modify the layout of the window to display more or less information and delete from the session regions that are no longer needed. The Audio and MIDI Region Lists combine to provide powerful and flexible editing possibilities that will be discussed further in Chapter 4, 'Editing'.

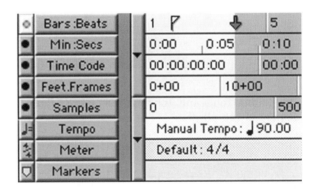

The Ruler provides the timing reference within a session

Time Formats

At the top of the edit window, one or more rulers are displayed. These provide the timing reference. The item Ruler View Shows in the Display window allows you to select the information you wish to be displayed along the time axis using one or a combination of the Timebase Rulers [Bars:Beats, Minutes:Seconds, Time Code (SMPTE-based), Feet:Frames (for 35mm film), Samples] and Conductor Rulers [Tempo (metronome setting), Meter (beat format) and user-defined position markers.] Any of the Timebase Rulers can be chosen to represent the Main Time Scale, which also serves as a basis for the Grid/Nudge and cursor functions (see Chapter 4,

'Editing'). An additional reference is provided by the Sub Location Indicator. You might use this, for example, to indicate the elapsed time in minutes and seconds whilst the Main Time Scale is displaying bar and beat numbers.

The Location Indicators display the current position in the Main and Sub Time Scales

Edit And Zoom

The Zoom Buttons and the Editing Tools along with the Event Edit Area combine to make possible precise editing of the events in the playlist.

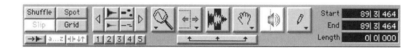

The Editing Tools and Zoom Buttons permit flexible editing and display of the playlists

Editing Functions

Although the Edit and Zoom functions are described in detail in Chapter 4, 'Editing', here's a brief overview.

- **Edit Mode Buttons** – These modes (Slip, Grid, Shuffle and Spot) determine the way regions behave within the playlist window as they are positioned, edited and moved around.

- **Zoom** – The horizontal and vertical zoom buttons allow you to enlarge or diminish the display of the data that interests you. The five preset buttons allow you to store and recall horizontal zoom values for audio and MIDI tracks.

- **Zoomer And Standard Trimmer** – Clicking or dragging with the Zoomer tool allows you to zoom in and out horizontally and/or vertically on data in the playlist. The Standard Trimmer can be used to resize regions or MIDI notes or scale the values for note velocities, controller events and automation breakpoints.

- **Selector And Time Grabber** – Data can be selected by dragging with the Selector in a track's playlist or in a Timebase Ruler. The Time Grabber can be used to select or move regions as well as MIDI and Conductor events. When a region or extract has been selected using the Selector, Trimmer or Grabber, the start and end points as well as the length of the selection are shown in the Event Edit Area.

- **Scrubber And Pencil** – The Scrubber allows you to play back audio data in either direction very slowly to identify errors or identify the exact location at which a cut is to be made, whilst the Pencil is used to insert MIDI notes or automation and controller events, edit MIDI velocities and repair audio waveforms (when zoomed down to sample level).

3 RECORDING WITH PRO TOOLS

Hard-disk recording systems such as Pro Tools, whilst retaining the imagery and much of the methodology of tape-based recording (whether on analogue reel-to-reels or modern digital multi-track recorders) represent an ingenious use of the possibilities of the computer in general, and random access storage in particular, to simplify many of the most wearisome tasks of editing, as well as offering musicians and recording engineers powerful new techniques and radically new ways of working that have changed forever how music is produced. Many processes that would have been difficult, if not impossible, or that would have involved considerable compromises in terms of sound quality, using analogue equipment, can be realized with very little effort and to achieve flawless results through the use of Pro Tools. The key to much of this is the concept of 'non-destructive editing'. Arrangements can be assembled from a host of disparate recordings and the material (apparently) reordered in time, duplicated, cut, corrected and modified in a multitude of other ways without the actual audio files from which the material is derived being altered in any way. Overdubbing is still possible, of course, and the technique of punching in and out to correct mistakes in isolated passages within a track is not new, but the seamless interweaving of a multitude of different takes, the effortless duplication of repeated material, the surgical precision with which mistakes can be identified and corrected without jeopardising the material that needs to be retained, and the ability to perform tasks that once required minutes of fiddly and painstaking work with a few simple mouse-clicks are all signs that a revolution in recording technology has taken place.

Preferences

Even though the basic functions of Pro Tools remain unaltered, users can adapt the system to suit their individual needs. After choosing Setups › Preferences and clicking Operation, you have the choice of determining how much of your available hard disk space is allocated for recording, by either limiting the recording time to a certain number of minutes or allocating the drive's entire available space (Allow Open-Ended Record Allocation). In the former case, once in the course of a recording the number of minutes you have specified is reached, Pro Tools will interrupt the recording and inform you of this fact or else that no more space is available on your hard disk for recording. In practice, limiting the recording time in this way is advisable, as it speeds up the recording process by reducing the overhead associated with disk allocation so that the Record command can be executed immediately.

Recording Options

Also on the Operations register card, you can select the option Latch Record Enable Buttons, which allows you to record-enable multiple tracks simply by clicking their Record Enable (rec) buttons one after the other. If you deselect this option, unless you shift-click the rec button, record-enabling one track automatically record-disables all the others to prevent you inadvertently 'recording over' a track you've just finished simply because you forgot to deselect its Record Enable button when you began work on the next track. It's true that unless you were working in destructive recording mode (see 'Recording Modes'), the original recording would not literally have been recorded over – it would still be there – but you might under certain circumstances lose editing done prior to the oversight.

Preparing To Record
I/O Settings

Prior to recording, whether in Pro Tools or on an analogue tape recorder, you have to assign the input and output channels through which the mixer will communicate with the recording device. In Pro Tools, these channels of communication are particularly easy to establish, since the mixer and recording device are one and the same. As described in chapter

2, 'The Basics', through the I/O Setup window, you can choose when creating a new session the channels your system will use for playing back as well as recording the data. Pro Tools offers preset configurations to link the inputs and outputs of your interfaces to the I/Os of the audio tracks, auxiliary inputs and master faders. Naturally you can also enter your own I/O settings – for a surround implementation, for example, or to create stereo inputs or outputs. Select I/O Setup from the Setup menu to configure the inputs, outputs, inserts and buses as well as any SampleCell cards and give them individual names if desired.

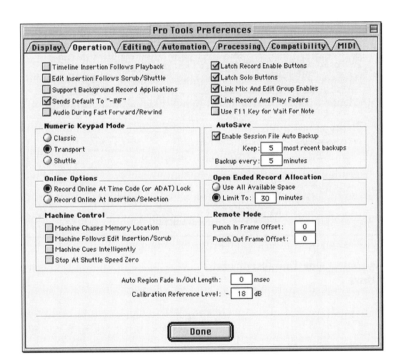

The I/O Setup window is used to configure the inputs and outputs for a session

When you next switch to the Edit or Mix windows, you will find the inputs and outputs now available for selection in the I/O section of each track. The current I/O settings will incidentally be retained for all subsequent sessions; the pop-up I/O settings in the New Session dialog box will display Last Used. You can, of course, choose another setup if you prefer.

File Locations

Just as important as the assignment of the audio inputs and outputs is deciding where to store the material you are about to record, since a new file will be created for every audio track. In the course of a Pro Tools session in 16-bit resolution at a sampling frequency of 44.1kHz, each audio track will consume around 5MB of space on your hard disk per minute. A 24-track recording will therefore generate 24 audio files and consume around 120MB of storage per minute. Since the average song lasts around three and a half minutes, you will need at least 420MB of disk space available before you begin, and bear in mind that with editing – especially if you are going to be doing a lot of overdubbing – you may end up using several times that amount. In fact, the current Pro Tools|HD system supports sampling frequencies as high as 192kHz, in which case a similar session to the one described would take up several gigabytes of disk space.

Heavy Demands On Disk Performance

The storage of data at this type of speed places heavy demands both on the hard disks and on the buss system of the computer that controls them. It is therefore advisable to share the workload of major productions between several hard disks, each of which must be capable of storing, locating and reading data at as high a speed as possible. In order to assign the storage locations for the audio tracks you're working on, open up the Disk Allocation dialog in the Setups menu.

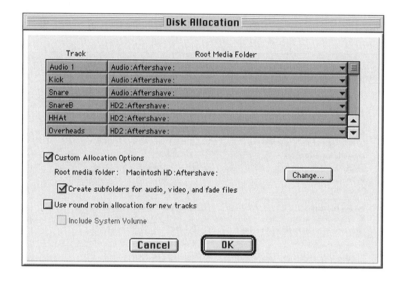

Using the Disk Allocation dialog, you can assign each track to a specific hard drive

Default Location

By default, Pro Tools stores all data in the root folder created along with the session and bearing its name. Within this folder, in addition to the session file, separate sub-folders are created for audio files, fade files and plug-in settings.

Disk Allocation

If your root folder is on your system hard drive, it is advisable to override the default and store the audio tracks elsewhere, as performance for audio recording and playback on system hard drives is inferior to that on other drives. Using the pop-up menus in the Record Drive column of the Disk Allocation dialog, you can

assign each track to a specific hard drive. Pro Tools will create a folder similar to the root folder on each new drive used and place the audio tracks assigned to it in a sub-folder, again named Audio Files. You have the option of letting Pro Tools allocate any future tracks you create to available drives on a round robin basis (Use Round Robin Allocation for New Tracks) as well as stipulating whether or not to include the system drive (Include System Volume) when doing so.

Monitoring

Once you have completed the In/Out and file allocation assignments, you can record-enable the requisite tracks using the buttons provided; the signal at the selected inputs will now be assigned to the appropriate track and heard over the mix/monitor sum according to your output routing assignments. It is possible to create a rough mix using the pan sliders and volume faders as well as loading the first plug-ins to add compression, equalisation or reverb to the monitor signal. This rough mix, of course, will only rarely satisfy the monitoring needs of the individual instrumentalists or singers, each of whom will require a mix that enables them to assess and control their own performance as they are recording. As Pro Tools operator, it is your job therefore to create a number of different sub-mixes for the various performers.

Track Sends

For this purpose, Pro Tools offers up to five mono or stereo sends per track, the signals of which can be taken either pre- or post-fader. For each foldback (ie monitor) mix, you need to create a stereo send in each track. In this case, it is better to use the pre-fader signal, as then you will be able to adjust the monitoring level independently of the output fader. The physical outputs should be connected to an external headphone amplifier. Using the Aux Sends controls, you can now set the level of the recording signal and determine its position in the stereo image independently of the track settings.

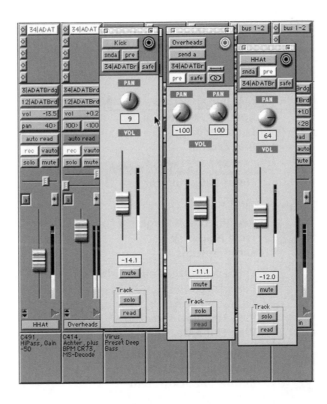

Use the Aux Sends to create a variety of foldback mixes for different hardware outputs

Monitoring Modes

The Monitor Mode is set globally for the entire session. As already mentioned, the input signals during recording are reproduced via the tracks in the Pro Tools mixer. You, like the musicians, monitor the input signal of the interface, which can be modified to suit individual needs by plug-ins and by adjusting track parameters. In Pro Tools, this mode is selected by checking Input Only Monitor in the Operations menu. Independently of the playback/recording status of your session, the monitor mix includes the input signals of all record-enabled tracks. In practice you should use this mode for live recording and the first take of your recording session.

Overdubbing

When you begin overdubbing (see 'Recording Modes'), you will need to switch monitoring modes. Overdubbing is the process of re-recording passages in an existing track, usually to correct mistakes. In such cases, the musician will want to listen to the material already recorded on the track prior to the punch-in point (when the fresh recording begins), but monitor the input signal thereafter. As soon as the punch-in point is reached, the monitor needs to switch automatically from playing back the track to monitoring the fresh input. In the Operations menu, selecting Auto Input Monitor deselects Input Only Monitor and vice versa.

Recording Modes

As with monitoring, Pro Tools offers a number of recording options. Of highest priority is Destructive Record in the Operations menu. In principle, Pro Tools is designed as a non-destructive editing and recording system, which means that all of the recorded audio data is preserved even though much of it may have been cut from or overwritten in the playlist; if you wish to restore any part of it at any time, you'll find it listed in the Regions list of the Edit window. This system offers a very high degree of protection against data loss and permits very flexible editing, but it also makes high demands upon the storage capacity of your disk drives. With each overdub, for example, a fresh recording of the passage is written to the disk, leaving the previous takes, so a track with a lot of overdubs might take up several times more disk space than a single take.

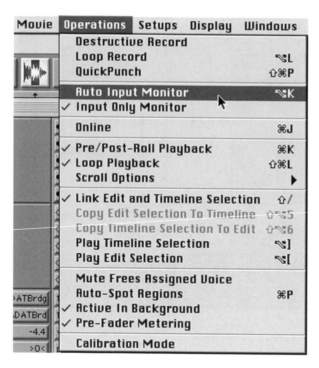

The choice of monitoring modes is determined by the recording situation

Destructive Recording

With the Destructive Record option, therefore, Pro Tools offers you the possibility of performing overdubs destructively like on an analogue reel-to-reel. This means that each new take erases the preceding one. The audio data that has been superseded is in this case lost forever, but since successive overdubs no longer take up additional disk space, the requirements of an overdubbed track are essentially the same as those of a track with no overdubbing. In practice, you should only make use of this option when establishing the framework of your session and when you are sure that you will have no further use for the discarded material. For subsequent overdubs, it is advisable to return to non-destructive mode, which allows you to compare successive takes and perhaps edit them.

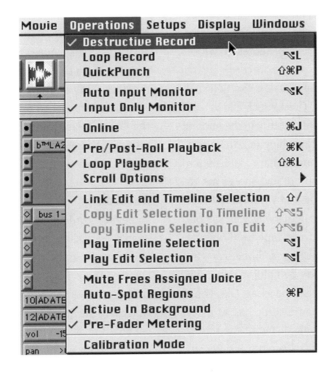

When Destructive Record is selected, each new take erases the one before it

Loop Recording

A further option specially designed for overdubbing is the Loop Record mode. Musicians find it useful sometimes to record a passage several times in quick succession, to try out different phrasing, for example. The passage to be looped is defined with the Selector in the ruler or in the track's playlist and displayed in the Event Edit Area at the top of the Edit window as well as in the Transport WINDOW (Display › Transport window Shows › Expanded). When you begin recording, the passage selected is recorded repeatedly with each pass creating a new entry in the Region list – the regions thus created being numbered incrementally. In the playlist, the most recent take is always the active one.

Comparing Takes

To listen to previous takes, select the active take in the Edit window using the Grabber. Then drag the recording you wish to hear from the Region List into the Playlist whilst holding down the Command key. The take is inserted with frame accuracy into the correct position in the Playlist. In this way you can listen to various takes one after the other.

Pre-Roll

When recording in Loop Record mode, prior to the first pass the performer may require to be given a musical cue (the bars leading up to the point at which he or she is to begin recording). This is called a 'pre-roll' and you can set its length. If enabled, the pre-roll is only heard prior to the first pass of the loop. The second and all successive passes commence as soon as the preceding pass ends. There is no Post-roll in Loop Record mode.

QuickPunch

The third option, QuickPunch mode, is another recording technique borrowed from tape-based recording. Unlike other Pro Tools procedures, in which the start, end and length of the recording are determined beforehand, perhaps using the Selector tool in the Playlist or Timeline, QuickPunch allows you to switch to Record Mode instantaneously in the middle of playback (this is known as 'punching in'), to correct an error in the existing recording perhaps, and switch back to Playback Mode ('punch out') when you get to the part of the existing recording that you wish to keep. You can correct up to 100 errors in this way, with sample accuracy, by punching in and out repeatedly in the course of a single take. In QuickPunch mode, you can switch to and from record mode by holding down the Command key and pressing the spacebar. Like Loop Mode, QuickPunch mode is non-destructive. At most one of the three recording modes listed at the top of the Operations menu (Destructive Record, Loop Record and QuickPunch) can be selected at any one time. If none is selected, Pro Tools defaults to the fourth mode, that is, normal, one-pass, non-destructive recording with a programmed starting point.

MIDI Recording

The recording of MIDI data is explained in detail in Chapter 6, 'Pro Tools And MIDI', but we would like to discuss briefly here the differences between the recording of audio and MIDI tracks. Basically, the recording of audio and MIDI data in Pro Tools is almost identical, the difference being limited to a few points.

Differences Between MIDI And Audio Recording

MIDI tracks serve to record MIDI messages (or commands). Compared with audio, such data takes up next-to-no space on your hard disk and rather than being stored in separate files in a separate folder, it is simply included in the session file. In the I/O section of your MIDI track, choose the input and output devices in your OMS setup.

No Sends Or Inserts

MIDI tracks offer neither inserts nor sends, as plug-ins and monitor outputs accept only audio data.

No Voices

MIDI tracks also make no claims upon the voices of your Pro Tools system. Instead of a Voice Selector, they therefore have a Program button (labelled P when the Track Height is set to Small), which is used to specify the Default Program Change – in other words, the program change message sent to the external MIDI module when the track is played.

Recording

To begin recording a MIDI track, you must first record-enable it by clicking on its rec button exactly as you would for an audio track. All MIDI messages from the selected input device are now routed to the selected OMS output. When you commence recording in the usual way using the Record and Play buttons in the Transport window, the recorded events are placed in a region that appears both in the playlist and in the MIDI Regions list. The monitor and recording modes in the Operations menu obviously have no bearing on MIDI tracks.

Destructive

Whether Destructive Record is or is not selected is also irrelevant, since all MIDI recording is destructive unless Loop Mode is engaged (this is discussed later). After recording a MIDI track, you can however discard the entire take using the Undo command in the Edit menu, which does have the effect of restoring the track's playlist to its prior state. You can also stipulate whether newly entered MIDI data be merged with, or replace, existing MIDI data on the track, by toggling the MIDI Merge button in the Transport window.

Loop Record Mode

In Loop Record mode, MIDI data is not recorded destructively; with each pass, a new region is created and added to the MIDI region list. Such regions can later be dragged to the playlist and played back.

It's not necessary to select QuickPunch to punch on the fly with MIDI tracks, as this is possible in both non-destructive and destructive recording modes.

Special Functions
Metronome Function

The MIDI controls include a metronome function, whereby a MIDI click is emitted at intervals determined by the Tempo Map in the Edit window. The tempo and time signature (or 'meter') are entered by selecting Display › Transport window Shows › MIDI controls and double-clicking the appropriate items. You can also select the note values for the click.

In combination with the MIDI functionality, it is possible to set the tempo and metre for your recording. The tempo is determined by Pro Tools' MIDI Metronome, which emits a MIDI click at intervals determined by the Tempo Map in the Edit window. First you must define a tempo and metre (time signature) for your session. To do this, activate the option Transport window Shows › MIDI Controls in the Display menu, set the tempo using the slider, and then, after double-clicking on the note icon, select a note value for the click. If you wish to change the time signature, either double-click on the Meter icon or select Change Meter in the MIDI menu. Should your recording involve complex tempo or time signature changes, activate the MIDI Conductor icon. When this option is active, you can enter time and tempo changes via the tempo map by selecting the point in the recording at which the change is to take effect (with

the Selector tool) and entering the new values in the Change Tempo and Change Meter dialogs accessed from the MIDI menu. During recording and playback, the metronome will automatically follow the tempo and metrical directions you have entered.

Activating The Click

Once you have set the tempo and metrical scheme, you need to configure and activate the click itself. To do this, open the Click/Countoff Options dialog (MIDI › Click Options), and choose whether you want the metronome to operate during both playback and recording, during recording only, or during the lead-in (Countoff) only. Next you must specify the OMS output to which the MIDI module that will produce the click is connected. You can then program the pitch, velocity and duration of both the accented and unaccented clicks.

Lead-in

For tempo-based recordings, it is helpful to be given the beat before you begin. To do this, check the Countoff field in the Countoff section of the dialog. By default, you are given a count-in of two bars though you can enter some other value if you prefer.

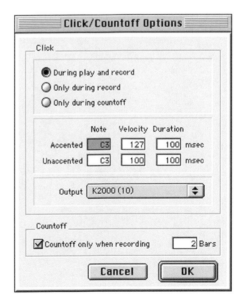

Determining when and how your MIDI metronome should sound

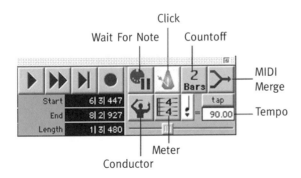

Tempo and time MIDI controls in the Transport bar

Recording
Laying Tracks

When you click on the Record button in the Transport window followed by the Play button, Pro Tools will commence recording on all record-enabled tracks. Unless you have pre-programmed a punch-out point, you will have to stop the recording manually, either by clicking the Stop button with the mouse or simply by pressing the spacebar. A new region, which will appear in both the playlist and either the Audio or the MIDI Region List, will have been created for the new audio data in each track.

Naming Files

Each new file is named automatically following a convention whereby the file name consists of the track name followed by the number of the take, the takes being numbered incrementally, beginning with 01. Since filenames begin with the name of the track, it is advisable to name all tracks prior to recording. Otherwise, new audio and MIDI files will be named according to the convention 'AudioX-Number' and 'MIDIX-Number' respectively, where 'X' represents the number of the track within the session. Bear in mind that by the time you come to edit, you may well have forgotten which instrument was on which track.

Recording Formats And Suffixes

When recording stereo or multi-channel tracks, remember that these are stored as split mono files. In the Regions List and on your hard disk, Pro Tools will add a suffix to indicate the stereo or surround assignment of the file in question. The left and right stereo channels are given the suffixes '.L' and '.R' respectively. The surround suffixes are more complex ('.L', '.R', '.LC', '.RC', '.C', '.LS', '.RS' and '.LFE').

4 EDITING

In this chapter, we will look at the role played by regions in Pro Tools, in what ways they can displayed in the Edit window and what lies behind the concepts Playlist and Regions List. You will learn the various Edit Modes and how zooming works in Pro Tools. To be able to work most effectively with Pro Tools, you need to make intelligent use of the scrolling options and know how to operate the Scrubber. Selection of the most appropriate tool for each task is the key to swift and efficient editing.

One of the great strengths of Pro Tools lies in the wealth of different techniques available to the recording editor. You can shorten regions, move them forwards or backwards in time, repeat them at will, add fades and so on. What's more, all the editing options we have listed are non-destructive – in other words, they leave the original audio file completely unaltered.

The Basics
Regions
Much of the time when editing, you will be working with regions, and first of all a distinction has to be made between audio and MIDI regions. Audio regions are essentially references to an existing audio file. The same region can, for example, appear in many different places in a session even though there is only one copy of the audio file to which each instance refers. You can also create many different regions that refer to different parts of the same audio file; again, Pro Tools does not need to copy the audio file. When you lay down a vocal track, for example, Pro Tools will initially create a single region that refers to the entire file you have just recorded – the entire take, if you like – and place it in the playlist of the track in question as well as entering its name in bold type in the Audio Regions List to indicate that it is a *whole file region*.

Whole file regions are by no means the only type of region. There are, for example, *user-defined regions* – the regions you create by shortening, splitting or editing whole file regions in other ways. *Multi-channel regions* appear as single regions in the Audio Regions List even though they refer to stereo or surround (ie multiple) audio files.

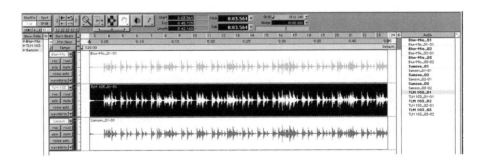

Regions that represent an entire audio file appear in bold type in the Audio Regions List

Track View

The type of data displayed in the Edit window and the size of the display are chosen by you on a track-by-track basis. For an audio track, you are offered a choice that includes blocks, waveform, volume, mute and any plug-in parameters that have been automated.

Audio tracks are normally set to *waveform view* – a graphic display of the amplitude of the signal. With a little practice, you will find that you can 'read' the audio file from this type of display, by which we mean 'find exactly the point you are looking for' to modify or make a cut.

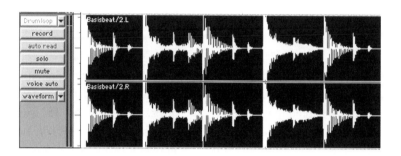

Practised users can 'read' the audio file just by looking at the waveform

Blocks

Set the display to *block view* when you have finished capturing and editing individual regions and begin moving or editing them, as well as whenever you are more interested in the speed at which the computer redraws the screen than the finer details of the amplitude. The other options come into their own primarily when you are editing automation data. To change the style of the display, click on the Track Display Format Selector and choose the option you require from the pop-up menu.

Pro Tools offers a variety of display formats for the track data

Aux And Master Fader Tracks

Fewer display options are available for auxiliary input tracks and master fader tracks than are available for audio tracks – you cannot, for example, display their waveforms.

MIDI Tracks

A different set of options are available for the display of MIDI track data. Most of the time, you will choose notes or regions, each of which displays notes in 'piano-roll' format. Select regions when arranging the order of, of joining together, regions. Select notes to add or edit individual notes. The other formats are for displaying various types of MIDI controller data with which you will seldom need to concern yourself.

Display Height

Regardless of whether it is an audio, MIDI, auxiliary input or master fader track, you can alter the height of its display by clicking either on the small arrow next to the display or in the area to the right of the track controls and choosing one of the six preset heights from the *Track Height* pop-up menu. The larger the display, obviously, the easier it is to see what you are doing when meticulous care is called for, but most of the time you will prefer to see a greater number of tracks, albeit in less detail, as this will give you a better overview of the session. For stereo or other multi-channel tracks, you have the option of displaying the playlists for each channel separately. Having access to each individual channel can be useful if you wish to create unusual stereo effects.

Audio Regions And Waveforms

The waveform display provides a great deal of information about the nature of the audio material in the region. For example, in the opposite illustration, depicting a drum loop, the sharpness of the peaks reflects the rapidity of the instrument's attack and decay.

Reading The Waveform

The greater the oscillation, the higher the amplitude – as soon as the volume drops off, a valley is formed between the peaks that indicate accents. With other instruments, depending, naturally, upon the way they are played, the waveform is likely to be less jagged. The drum loop, however, is useful for illustrating one of the golden rules of editing: try always to make your cuts immediately before a peak for two reasons: firstly it will help to ensure that an even rhythm is maintained when edited regions are arranged one after another in the playlist, and secondly, by making cuts in places where the volume level is at its lowest, you will avoid the clicks and pops that occur when cuts are made elsewhere. Once again it must be emphasised that such cuts in no way damage or even effect the audio file itself. When editing regions, you are simply revising your instructions as to which parts of the audio files on the hard disk Pro Tools should read during playback and in what order.

Playlists
Multiple Playlists

The *playlist* determines the order in which the various regions of which a track is composed are played back. To allow maximum freedom for experimentation, you can create alternative playlists for the same track and choose the one that works best. You cannot, of course, play back more than one playlist for the same track at the same time.

Automation Playlists

Each audio track has its own *automation playlists*, since the automation data is contained not in the regions themselves but in the tracks. By making multiple copies of the same audio playlist, you can try out different automation (eg volume and panning levels) on the same set of regions. When you first create a track, of course, the playlist is empty. It is only when you record something on it or drag regions into it from the regions lists that there is anything there to play back. When you delete a track from your session, you can either delete its playlists or use them in other tracks.

Region Lists
Inventory

Unlike the playlists, the *Region lists* are not part of your arrangement. They simply provide an inventory of all the regions – all the snippets of audio data – that are

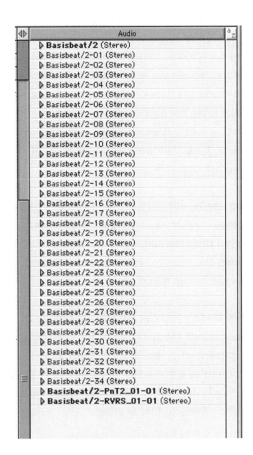

The Region List, where Regions and audio files are managed

available to you for the creation of your arrangement. On the right hand side of the Edit window, you will see that there are separate lists for audio regions and MIDI regions. It is possible to alter the size of the display. Using the pop-up menu at the top of each list, you can also sort the regions according to various criteria, elect to display or not display file, disk and path names, select, rename and clear regions from the session as well as importing or exporting data.

Edit Modes

The behaviour of the regions as you move them around within the Edit window varies depending upon the *edit mode* selected. Edit modes affect not only the movement and positioning of audio and MIDI regions (including individual MIDI notes) but also the effect of the copy and paste functions and that of the Trimmer, Selector, Grabber and Pencil. Here's a breakdown of the modes:

- **Shuffle Mode** – In shuffle mode, no two regions can overlap but nor can gaps appear between regions – each follows immediately from the one before. If a region is inserted at the beginning of the track, the other regions move to the right to make room for it (their playback is postponed, in other words); if an enclosed region is removed, the regions that were on either side of it snap together to fill the gap.

- **Slip Mode** – In slip mode, gaps are permitted between regions and regions can also overlap. One region can even completely cover another. Since it allows the greatest freedom, many editors prefer to work in slip mode.

- **Spot Mode** – You can think of spot mode as 'post-production' mode. It provides for the precise alignment of a region (or a specific sonic event within it) to a given SMPTE frame and is designed primarily for the synchronisation of music and sound effects to film or video.

- **Grid Mode** – In grid mode, you can define a grid such that when it is dragged into the playlist and released, the beginning of a region automatically

'snaps' to the nearest line of the grid. MIDI notes, too, that lie between lines can be quantized – in other words, directed to move to the nearest line. If you wish to tidy up the tempo of a sloppily played passage, for example, you can set the Main Time Scale to Bars:Beats and then quantize. You can even display the grid in the background like the lines on graph paper.

PRACTICAL TIP

To toggle the display of grid lines, hold down the Option key (Mac) or Alt key (Windows) and click on one of the rulers above the playlist window.

Zooming

The *horizontal* and *vertical zoom* functions allow you to adjust the scale of the display to the requirements of the moment. Of the two, the horizontal zoom function (which operates on the time axis) is the more useful. If you want a good overview of the entire session from beginning to end so that you can see all the successive regions at once, zoom out horizontally. Once you have decided where you wish to intervene – to fix an error, for example – you will need obviously to zoom back in so that you have enough detail to see what you are doing. In Pro Tools, it is possible to zoom in so tightly that a single sample occupies the entire breadth of the screen. At 44.1kHz, this is equivalent to one 40,000th of a second. Micro-surgery, you might say.

Vertical zoom affects only the contents of the regions as the tracks retain the height assigned them by the Track Height Selector. Different vertical zoom buttons are provided for Audio and MIDI regions. In practice, however, this function is useful only for rarely needed operations such as the elimination of pops and clicks using the Pencil tool. The horizontal zoom on the other hand, is useful in all kinds of contexts.

PRACTICAL TIP

Since you are likely to use if often, take a moment to memorise the keyboard shortcuts for the horizontal zoom function. On the Macintosh: Apple + [(open square bracket) to zoom in and Apple + [(close square bracket) to zoom out. On the PC, there's no Apple key so the Control key (Ctrl) is used instead.

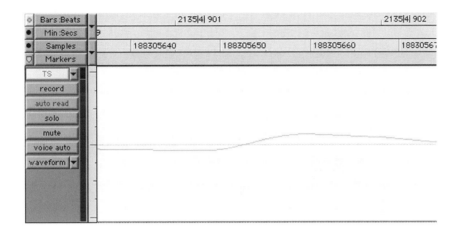

If need be, you can edit a single sample in Pro Tools

Preparing To Edit

Before you begin editing in Pro Tools, make sure you listen carefully to the entire track or at least to the passage you suspect requires work. Once you have identified the region, or the instant within a region, where you plan to intervene, you need to ensure that while you are working you can commence and recommence playback at precisely the right point so that you aren't constantly wasting time listening to bars that don't interest you whilst waiting for the ones that do.

The Playback Cursor

The *playback cursor* is a solid, unblinking line running from the top of the Edit window to the bottom. It moves across the screen from left to right indicating precisely the point playback has reached at any moment. Whether or not the playback cursor is visible depends upon the scrolling options.

The Edit Cursor

As soon as playback stops, the playback cursor becomes the *edit cursor* and begins to blink. The edit cursor marks the start point for whatever editing tasks you might undertake.

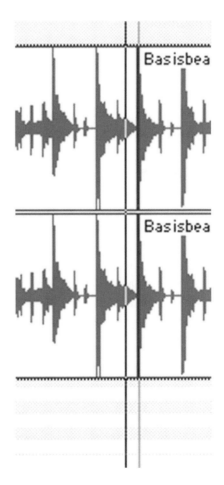

The vertical line indicates the point in the waveform playback has reached

Clicking Saves Time

Whilst you could obviously use the Play and Stop keys in the Transport window to set the playback position, it is far faster to just click the point in the track where you wish playback to begin. Instead of using the Play button in the Transport window, is usually easier to use the spacebar. Pressing the spacebar a second time will stop playback.

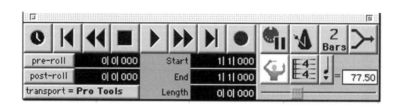

The controls in the Transport window are modelled on those of a cassette recorder

Location Indicators
Current Position

The current playback position is not only displayed in the Timeline but also by the location indicators at the top of the screen and in the Transport window.[Display > Transport window Shows > Counters] In each case, the format of the display is the same as that selected in the Timeline.

Scrolling Options

Pro Tools allows you to stipulate whether or not you wish the Edit window to scroll during playback. Set to No Auto-Scrolling, the cursor will stop when it reaches the right hand side of the screen and the display will not be refreshed. In practice, the option whereby Pro Tools redraws the screen to reflect the current location each time the cursor reaches the right hand edge (Operations > Scroll Options> Page Scroll During Playback) is far more helpful.

Scrubbing

The idea behind the Scrubber derives from a technique much used by audio engineers in the days of reel-to-reel tape, when they would move the tape slowly forwards and backwards over the playback head of the tape recorder to find the exact place where they wanted to cut the tape. In Pro Tools, the scrubbing speed is freely selectable. To get to the right general area, expert users often move at high speed through the track until they get close to the correct spot, at which point they slow to a crawl. In Pro Tools, you cannot scrub more than eight tracks at a time. Usually scrubbing is performed at the normal playback speed or slower, but in *scrub/shuttle mode* it is possible to scrub at high speed. To perform scrubbing, select the Scrubber tool and hold down the mouse button as you move the tool over the track. To switch to Scrub/Shuttle mode, hold down the Alt key (Windows) or Option key (Mac) as you do so.

The Toolbox

In Pro Tools, the effect of mouse movements varies depending upon the tool selected. Often the function of a tool is obvious from its very name but in other cases further explanation may be required. The Selector, for example, performs pretty much the services you would expect, whereas the Scrubber may surprise (though we hope not disappoint) in this respect. Understanding the proper function of each tool and when to use it will considerably ease the task of editing in Pro Tools. A particularly useful weapon is the so-called Smart Tool, which changes function depending upon the part of a region in which it finds itself. Here's a breakdown of the tools you'll find in the Toolbox:

- **Trimmer** – The *Standard Trimmer* is used to modify the length of a region. To reverse the direction of the cursor, which determines whether the start or end point is edited, Macintosh users should hold down the Option key and Windows users the Alt key. The Trimmer can also be used to *scale* (that is, to reduce or increase) the velocity of MIDI notes, controller data and automation breakpoints. TDM systems offer in addition a Scrub Trimmer, which allows you to listen to the audio material in Scrub mode while searching for the trim point, and the TCE Trimmer, which expands or shrinks the audio material within the region to fit the time range.

- **Selector** – The *Selector* is the most important tool for performing basic editing tasks in Pro Tools. If you hold down the mouse button and move the selector over a playlist, the result is an *edit selection*, which means that the editing operations that ensue will effect only the track material selected; drag the mouse in the same way over a timebase ruler and the result is a *timeline selection*, which selects all material on all tracks between the start and end points of the selection.

- **Grabber** – Clicking with the *Time Grabber* anywhere within a region, selects and permits you to move the entire region. It can also be used to select and move MIDI and conductor events. It can also be used for other tasks, such as the editing and insertion of automation breakpoints and to delete tempo and meter events. To delete automation breakpoints, hold down the Option key (Mac) or Alt key (Windows) and click. The Separation Grabber, as we have mentioned, is used to separate sections into new regions.

- **Scrubber** – The *Scrubber* is useful for locating aurally the precise point at which you wish to make a cut. The resolution is determined by the zoom level and the distance and speed at which you drag the tool determine the speed at which the audio plays back as well as the length of the passage heard.

- **Pencil** – The *Pencil* is used for the insertion of MIDI notes as well as for drawing in automation and controller data. When the display is zoomed in to

sample level, the Pencil is also useful for tasks such as the repairing of audio waveforms. When the Alt (Windows) or Option (Mac) keys are held down, the Pencil becomes an eraser and can be used to delete individual notes and controller or automation data. The effect is therefore like twiddling one of those old-fashioned pencil/erasers with the point at one end and the rubber at the other – you draw with the tip and erase with the top. When entering automation and controller data, a pop-up menu allows you to select between five shapes (Free Hand, Line, Triangle, Square and Random).

- **Smart Tool** – The function of the *Smart Tool* depends upon its position relative to the region or note you are editing. If placed at the beginning or end of a region, it operates as a standard Trimmer. If you move it to the transition between two regions, you can use it to perform crossfade.

- **Zoomer** – In addition to the zoom buttons and keyboard shortcuts, Pro Tools offers the *Zoomer* as a third way of accessing its horizontal and vertical zoom functions.

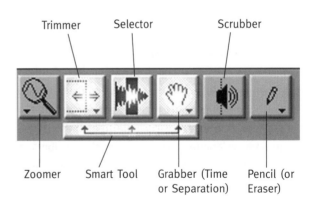

The Pro Tools toolbox

Editing Regions

Once you have made the necessary preparations and acquainted yourself with the most important tools, the actual work of editing can commence. Editing nowadays is one of the most important tasks in music production, since as a rule considerably more time is devoted to editing the recorded material than to the task of recording itself. The possibilities are now so extensive, that it is far from unknown for users to become so fascinated by the whole process that they forget why they are doing it. It is important, therefore, never to lose sight of the big picture and only to intervene where it is really necessary. For practice purposes, and while you are finding out how everything works, naturally everything is permitted, but when the work begins in earnest, it is important to keep the play instinct in check.

Topping And Tailing

One of the most important skills to acquire is being able to cut cleanly, so that no unwanted noise or rhythmic irregularity spoils the transition between regions. To this end, employ the Trimmer, and make sure that the correct edit mode has been selected, so that regions on different tracks do not drift out of sync and the tempo does not break down at the frontiers between regions. Fortunately Pro Tools offers *time stamping*, which means that every region recorded online is stamped with the SMPTE time at which the audio was originally recorded. With the help of the appropriate option in the Display menu, you can restore displaced regions quickly to their original positions.

Splitting Up Your Work

If, instead of simply trimming unwanted material from the start or end of a region, you wish to divide it into two or three pieces, this is most easily done using the Smart Tool. Suppose, for example, that there is one particularly well-performed passage within a region that you wish to use again elsewhere in the arrangement. Position the cursor over the middle of the region in the upper half (the Smart Tool becomes the Selector) and select the part of the region that you wish to copy. Now move the mouse downwards so that the Selector turns into a Grabber. Hold down the Option key (Macintosh) or Alt key (Windows) and drag the selection into another track. Immediately a new region is created bearing the name of the audio file but with a new region number. If instead of copying, you wish to cut the selected passage, drag the selection to another track as before but without holding down Alt or Option key.

Move And Copy

Moving and copying regions are two of the easiest tasks in Pro Tools. If you wish to move a region, select it with the Object Grabber and drag it to a new location. If you wish to copy it, select it with the Object Grabber whilst holding down the Option (Macintosh) or Alt (Windows) key.

Fades

The fade functions in Pro Tools are enormously powerful. We are not speaking hear of the fade-outs at the end of a piece of music; long drawn-out fades such as those are more easily created using Pro Tools' high-resolution automation. The type of fades we are talking about here are usually very short and serve mainly to ensure a smooth transition between two regions. These we will call *crossfades* but it is also possible to create fades at the beginning or end of regions that are not preceded or followed by other regions, and these are called, respectively, *fade-ins* and *fade-outs*.

When it comes to the geometry of crossfades, Pro Tools offers a wide variety of parameters to tinker with and tweak, but just accepting the defaults will yield perfectly satisfactory results in most situations. To create a crossfade, select an extract of any length at the transition between two regions and select in the Edit menu the entry Create Fades. The window that opens offers various options that allow you to tailor the geometry of the crossfade to your own requirements. By clicking on the Speaker icon in the top left hand corner, you can audition the fade.

In the case of a fade-in, select an area that extends to the exact beginning of the region or to a blank area in the track just prior to the beginning of the region. In the case of a fade-out, the selection must extend to the exact end or to a blank area beyond the end of the region. These limitations aside, the procedure is the same as for the creation of a crossfade.

Other Editing Functions

In addition to the basic editing functions, Pro Tools offers other highly practical functions that can save you a great deal of time and allow you to manipulate audio as freely MIDI.

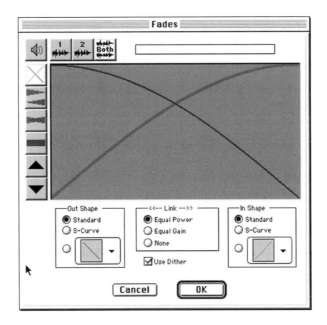

Pro Tools' crossfade function is powerful and flexible

Strip Silence

The *Strip Silence* function analyses the amplitude of the selected audio material, chopping it up into small regions and discarding from the Edit window all regions that conform to a particular definition of 'silence'. The selection may extend over several tracks and regions. This function is especially useful when you wish, for example, to quantize audio material or synchronise sound effects with precision using SMPTE. The function is also useful in conjunction with the Compact Selected command, which is used to optimise audio files and remove superfluous data from the hard disk.

To use the Strip Silence function, select Show Strip Silence from the Windows menu. In the window that opens, you are invited to define what should, and what should not, be considered an area of silence. Essentially this involves specifying a level and, with it, the length of time the amplitude of the signal must remain below that level for the passage to be considered silent. Momentary silences, in other words, can, if you wish, be disregarded. You may also wish to preserve small portions of the original audio that precede (pre-roll) or follow (post-roll) the retained regions, so as to avoid losing the characteristic starting and ending transients of particular instruments or the human voice. If so, you can specify their length.

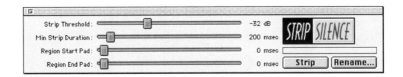

In the Strip Silence window, you can define the level beneath which audio material is to be considered silent

Consolidate Selection

Use this function when you have finished editing a track that comprises a large number of short regions with a large number of fades. When the command is executed, Pro Tools creates from these regions a single audio file that contains all the modifications you have made to the regions and all the crossfades but does not include any automation or plug-in data. This allows your disk drive to read the data more efficiently, as it is now dealing with a continuous audio file instead of jumping around looking for small snippets of audio stored in different parts of the hard disk. Select the passage from which you wish to create a new audio file and select Consolidate Selection from the Edit menu.

Compact Selected

This command is used to tidy up your hard disk and reduce the size of an audio file in which there are sections that have been discarded. Since this is a function that does relates to the original audio files, it is found in the Audio Regions List menu. This command is destructive as it results in the deletion of parts of the original audio file, which are then irrevocably lost. It is therefore a function best used with care.

The Beat Detective

The Beat Detective is only available with Pro Tools TDM systems. It works by identifying short peaks in the level of the selected audio, so that you can either extract the tempo information from the audio file or adapt the audio material to the tempo map of the session. This function is suitable for synchronising drum loops with MIDI tracks, either by forcing the MIDI tracks to follow the drum loop or the other way around. This function is found in the Windows menu. Experiment with it and you will learn not only its possibilities but also its limitations.

5 PLUG-INS

The quality of the available plug-ins and the range of different plug-in interfaces it provides are among the reasons Pro Tools systems have established themselves so successfully in the profession. Plug-ins are small programs, which – in our case – considerably increase the power and versatility of the Pro Tools software. The range includes effects such as reverb, chorus and delay as well as dynamic processors (compressors, expanders, limiters and so on) and special algorithms such as intonation aids and pitch-shifting/time-compression tools. When you buy a Pro Tools system, a certain number of plug-ins are included in the package, such as the DigiRack plug-ins produced by Digidesign itself. There are also however a multitude of very high-quality plug-ins from third-party suppliers on the market. At the end of the chapter, you will find a comprehensive overview of what is available in each area.

Plug-in Interfaces
Pro Tools Integration

The Pro Tools software integrates four different plug-in interfaces: AudioSuite, RTAS (Real-Time AudioSuite), TDM (Time Division Multiplexing) and HTDM (Host TDM). The TDM and HTDM interfaces are, of course, reserved for the large Pro Tools systems that offer TDM; Pro Tools LE and Free do not. Plug-ins are generally designed for a particular plug-in interface and incompatible with the others. An exception to this rule is provided by those TDM and HTDM plug-ins with which an RTAS version is thrown in at no extra cost – it doesn't happen the other way about. In such cases, the plug-in appears as a single entity in the Plug-ins folder, even though it can be used with both the TDM and the RTAS interfaces.

TDM Plug-ins

The processing for these plug-ins is performed on the digital signal processors of the TDM cards, which only the TDM systems offer. With Pro Tools LE or Free, there is no TDM interface.

AudioSuite Plug-ins

The AudioSuite interface differs from the others in that it does not operate in real time but is used to modify audio files on the hard disk. Select all or part of one or more regions and choose a plug-in from the AudioSuite menu. The output of an AudioSuite plug-in, which uses the power of the host CPU to do its processing, is written directly to the hard disk either as a new file or by overwriting the original audio file. There is, however, a Preview function that will allow you to check your settings before making any drastic changes.

RTAS

This interface is primarily designed for use with the host-based Pro Tools systems such as Digi001, Digi002, Mbox and Audiomedia III that are supplied with Pro Tools LE. RTAS is a real-time plug-in interface that uses the CPU of the host computer for its processing requirements. When used with TDM systems, the RTAS interface is subject to certain limitations: firstly, RTAS plug-ins can only be used in audio tracks, not in auxiliary input tracks or master faders; secondly, if you want to use TDM and RTAS plug-ins in the same audio track, the RTAS plug-ins must be placed before the TDM ones in the signal chain; and thirdly, the audio track must be switched to Voice Auto.

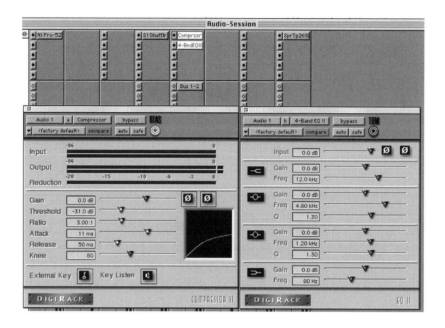

In TDM systems, you can use RTAS and TDM plug-ins in the same channel strip

HTDM

This interface was primarily designed for software tone generators, which although they employ the host-CPU are nonetheless capable of being directly integrated into the TDM mixing console. Unlike RTAS-based software tone generators, HTDM plug-ins can also be used with auxiliary input tracks, so no audio tracks need to be sacrificed.

Plug-in Uses And The Aux Principle

If you wish to use a plug-in in a Pro Tools session, it has to be introduced into the signal path – it must, so to speak, be 'inserted'. Each such use of a plug-in within a session is described as an 'instance'. A plug-in is selected and inserted into the signal chain of an audio track, auxiliary input track or master fader via the Inserts section, which is found at the top of the channel strip in Pro Tools' Mix window. If you use several plug-ins in a single track, the signal flow runs from the highest placed (in the channel strip) to the lowest. Since the inserts come before the fader in the signal chain, the position of the fader has no effect upon the level of the signal processed by the plug-ins;

the inserts, in other words, are switched *pre-fader*, except on master fader tracks, which are *post-fader*.

The Insert Principle

In Pro Tools, plug-ins mostly operate on the *insert* principle; an insert is a loop introduced into the signal path of a channel that diverts the entire signal of that channel into a hardware or (in this case) software effects device and then routes it back into the channel. In this way, the signal of a single channel might pass successively through a compressor, an equaliser and a number of other plug-ins of the type that act upon the entire signal of a channel. There are other effects, however, such as reverb and chorus, that are designed merely to add something (a *wet,* in other words, processed signal), leaving the source (the *dry* signal) unchanged. If you wish to use a plug-in of this type in the Inserts section of the channel strip, it needs to be equipped with a Wet/Dry control so that you can vary the dosage of the effect.

The Auxiliary Principle

Although auxiliary input tracks can be used in a wide range of contexts within Pro Tools, their primary

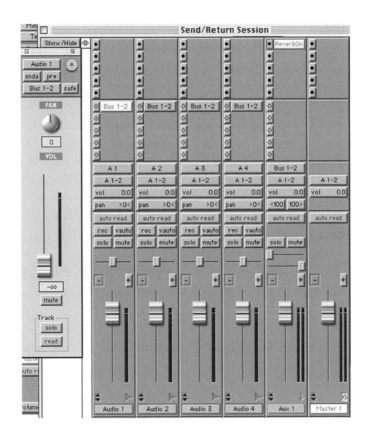

In this illustration, audio tracks 1–4 are sharing a single reverb (the plug-in in Aux 1). All four are sending part of their signal via Buss 1–2 to Aux 1, which adds the reverb and sends the result to stereo output A 1–2

function is that of effects sends. The advantage of using an auxiliary input (as opposed to an insert) is that the same plug-in instance can be used for several audio tracks at the same time, sparing the resources of the system.

In the standard configuration, the input of an auxiliary input channel is set to Buss 1–2 (for example) and its output to the stereo sum (A 1–2). The next step is to put a reverb plug-in in the auxiliary input channel's first Insert slot and select the desired preset. Take care to set the plug-in to output only the wet signal. The next step is to add a send to each of the channels to which you wish to add reverb, in each case clicking the Send Destination button and selecting Buss 1–2, which, you will remember, is the input of the Aux Send channel with the reverb in it.

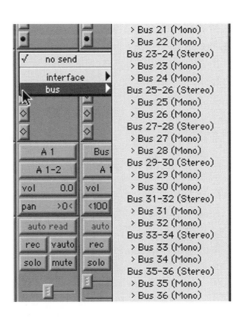

The Send Destination may be either one of the internal mix busses or a hardware I/O

Plug-ins In Practice

In practice, plug-ins raise a number of questions relating to latency and the availability of multi-channel instances (stereo or surround formats) as well as to operation and automation.

Latency

Digital signal processing is inevitably associated with a certain degree of latency. It becomes a problem when a plug-in is applied to only one of several tracks that are running in parallel. Depending upon the degree of latency, this can result in phase cancellation and, in severe cases, a noticeable loss of synchronicity between different tracks. The amount of latency introduced into the signal path by a plug-in is a function of the speed of the processor and the complexity of the algorithm.

Since the DSPs of TDM systems are specially designed for the processing of audio data and are therefore the ideal processors for this type of application, the latency of many TDM plug-ins is no more than a few samples and can therefore be ignored most of the time.

The CPU of a computer, on the other hand, has to perform a large number of tasks simultaneously, which is why the degree of latency introduced by CPU-based real-time plug-ins (RTAS) is generally higher. Pro Tools automatically resolves the timing problems introduced by RTAS plug-ins during playback. One snag with them, though, is that they cannot be used when recording – at least, not in the tracks that are being recorded.

In TDM systems, instances of latency can be displayed and corrected either using the Time Adjuster plug-in or manually. Click twice on the Track Level Indicator in a Mix window channel strip and Pro Tools will display the latency of the channel in samples. To compensate for this latency, you can use the Time Adjuster plug-in to delay the other channels by the same amount. It's often simpler, in the case of audio tracks is simply to move all the regions of the affected track to the left (that is, forwards in time) by the same amount, bringing it back into sync with the rest of the tracks.

Multi-Channel Plug-ins

Pro Tools offers a number of different ways of implementing multi-channel plug-ins, the simplest case being a stereo plug-in, specifically designed for insertion into a stereo track. If no stereo version of a particular plug-in exists – which is unusual – there remains the possibility of using multiple mono instances to achieve the same result. This is certainly the favoured solution for surround channels, since there are very few plug-ins on the market specifically designed for multi-channel signal processing.

The Plug-in Window

Every plug-in has an individual user interface, however the top panel of every plug-in window is the same, and it is here that you will find the basic functions

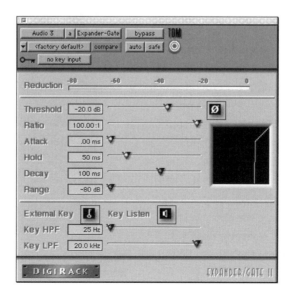

The top panel of all plug-in windows offers the same functions

as well as access to the supplied presets. These include a Bypass button, used to remove the plug-in from the signal chain; a Compare button, which toggles between the current settings and the preset, affording you the opportunity of judging to what extent, if any, the changes you have just made have improved the sound; an auto button, which creates an automation playlist for the selected parameter, so that you can control it using Pro Tools' automation; and a Key Input, which is used to feed a control signal (known as a side chain) from an input or buss into the control path of the plug-in. This button obviously is only visible if the plug-in offers this feature, as many dynamics plug-ins do.

Plug-in Settings And Presets

In Pro Tools, plug-ins are stored in the DAE folder along with their settings, meaning the factory presets with which the plug-ins are delivered. If you create new presets during a session, these can be stored in a separate Plug-in Settings sub-folder in the session folder. The Settings menu, accessed via the arrow to the left of the Librarian menu at the bottom left of the panel, allows you to copy, paste, save and import plug-in settings. Mac users, who now have access to a vast arsenal of plug-ins, should increase the amount of RAM assigned to DAE (Pro Tools 5.1.1 or earlier). Around 100MB is normal. For RTAS plug-ins to deliver their true potential, a few settings in the Playback Engine Setup dialog need to be changed.

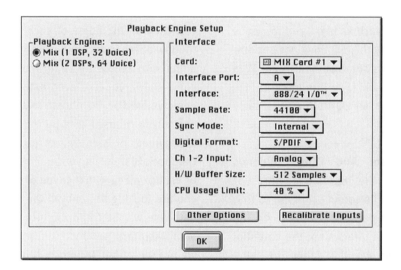

The Playback Engine Setup dialog allows you to fine-tune your system

The Digidesign presets represent a sensible compromise between the twin demands of power and user-friendliness. If you find that your CPU cannot process any more RTAS plug-ins, you can still squeeze a little more out of the system by raising the CPU Usage Limit to 85 per cent as well as increasing the H/W Buffer Size. Both of these measures have their drawbacks, however, as increasing the former can result in sluggish graphics, whilst increasing the latter will increase the latency of the system.

The Foundation Bundle

A selection of plug-ins, designed to satisfy all your fundamental recording needs, is bundled with all Pro Tools software. This is not to be confused with the constantly changing assortment of promotions from third-party suppliers that varies in scope and quality depending upon the hardware you buy.

The foundation bundle is just that – it provides a sound basis upon which to build, but it has to be said that the EQ plug-ins bundled with Pro Tools cannot really compete with some of the other EQ plug-ins on the market, and the same goes for the dynamic processors. The various delays perform well and many of the miscellaneous AudioSuite functions – such as time stretching, pitch shifting, normalisation, reverse and DC offset removal – do a pretty decent job.

Here are the most important of the real-time plug-ins bundled with Pro Tools:

- **DigiRack EQ** – The EQ comes in two useful versions: the first is a classical four-band EQ such as that offered by numerous analogue mixing consoles and the second, a flexible single-band EQ offering different types of filter. Whilst the four-band EQ is designed to add EQ in the normal way to a track, the single-band EQ allows more drastic interventions such as high- and low-pass filtering. Unfortunately this EQ does not perform anything like as well as some of the RTAS or TDM EQ plug-ins on the market, so it is more or less obligatory to invest in an EQ from a third-party supplier.

- **DigiRack Compressor And Other Dynamic Processors** – Whilst the bundled compressor performs respectably, its sound is inferior to that of certain other third-party compressors on the market, even though it offers all of the essential parameters and displays. It is much the same story with the Limiter, Gate and DeEsser: in each case, there is a third-party plug-in that does the same job but much better than the DigiRack version. In fairness it must be said that the DigiRack Expander works very well and can be recommended without hesitation.

- **DigiRack Delay** – The delay comes in four different versions that differ essentially in their maximum delay times. These plug-ins function flawlessly and are perfectly adequate for simple delay effects. However, if you need more modulation possibilities, delay instances or the simulation of analogue echo devices, you have no option but to resort to a third-party supplier.

Recommended Plug-ins

Without making any claim to comprehensiveness, in the following sections we would like to draw your attention to some of our favourite plug-ins in the principal categories. Whilst this is intended to help you decide where to invest, it is also a good idea to check out the demo versions on the internet pages of the various software houses that produce plug-ins. You are usually allowed to try out fully functional versions of these plug-ins for a limited period, so that you can decide for yourself whether or not they deliver anything you really need. To get an overview of what is on offer, a good place to start is the Plug-In Info page accessed via the Distributors page at the Digidesign website at www.digidesign.com, where you will find the available plug-ins listed alphabetically along with the name of the supplier, the price and a brief description; when you click on the name of each plug-in an Overview window opens in which you will find a fuller description along with access to its technical specifications. In some cases, you can even listen to, or download a demo version of, the plug-in that interests you before committing yourself to a purchase. A search function is provided for each system (eg Pro Tools|24 Mix or Digi 001); just select your operating system from the os list box along with the type of effect (eg Guitar Amp) you are looking for, and all the available plug-ins of that type will be listed. Unfortunately not all plug-in manufacturers support the Windows platform as vigorously as the Macintosh, though this is changing, and it is worth checking the site regularly to keep abreast of developments.

Dynamics

There are a large number of suppliers with different offerings in this area, notable among them Focusrite, Waves and McDSP. From the point of view of sound, we liked the McDSP Compressor Bank and the Waves Renaissance Compressor best, each of which is available for both RTAS and TDM. The Compressor Bank is also very resource-friendly and makes very few demands upon the CPU or your TDM chips. If you need dynamics in order to maximise loudness, either the L1 or the newer L2, both from Waves, would make an excellent choice.

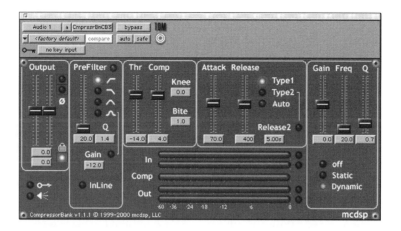

The McDSP Compressor Bank – outstanding sound and resource-friendly

Equalisers

Here, too, there are plug-ins for both RTAS and TDM from Focusrite, Waves and McDSP. There is also the superb Sony Oxford EQ plug-in plus Massenburg Option, which satisfies the highest demands in terms both of sound quality and processing overhead. This plug-in is only available for TDM systems. You can also obtain outstanding sound from both the Filter Bank from McDSP and the Renaissance EQ from Waves. The Filter Bank is especially to be commended for its economical use of resources.

Reverb

With reverb, a clear distinction has to be made between RTAS and TDM, the choice of plug-ins available for RTAS is very limited. Once again, the offering here in the Waves Renaissance series is very popular. Also in the RTAS category, the Altiverb from Audio Ease with its 'impulse response' presets has a very good sound, however this type of stereo reverb has a tendency to overtax the current crop of computers. Post-production tasks on the other hand are best managed with Real Verb from Kind of Loud (RTAS and TDM). In the TDM market, Digidesign itself is well placed with the Reverb One, competitors being the somewhat greying LexiVerb, Mega Reverb from TC Works and naturally also the Renaissance Reverb from Waves. In TDM systems, the reverb should generally be handled by TDM plug-ins, since RTAS plug-ins

cannot be used in TDM aux input tracks, which rules out a send/return configuration.

Multi-Band Dynamics

Here the C4 from Waves competes with the MC 2000 from McDSP and MasterX from TC Works, the first being also available for the RTAS platform. These plug-ins are especially well suited to the task of processing the master fader or instrument groups. Unlike normal wide-band compressors, multi-band compressors allow you to apply different – and perhaps quite drastic – dynamic processing to different wave bands. Each of the three has its special merits, with MasterX being particularly convincing in the main mix, since a single instance buys you three dynamics units (expander, compressor and limiter). Many users, however, swear by the sound of the C4 or MC 2000.

Delay

If the simple delay effects of the supplied Digidesign plug-ins are not sufficient for your purposes, there are a few attractive delay plug-ins available from other suppliers. The Super Tap from Waves, an outstanding six-voice multi-tap delay plug-in with a maximum delay time of up to six seconds, has things pretty much its own way in the RTAS field. For TDM systems, as well as the Waves offering just discussed, the Echo Farm from Line 6 is to be recommended. This plug-in simulates numerous vintage echo devices, including the Roland Space Echo RE-101, Maestro EP-1 and EP-3, and sounds great.

Modulation Effects

The choice of effects here includes the Mondo Mod and Meta Flanger from Waves and the TC Chorus from TC Works. Whilst the TC Chorus does provide the TDM mixer with a classic chorus effect, the Waves offerings are considerably more flexible and they are also available for RTAS. The plug-ins from Wave Mechanics have also made a name for themselves for their somewhat weird modulation effects; both the Time Bender and Pitch Bender, however, are only available as TDM plug-ins.

Pitch Correction

The Antares Auto-Tune, which was the first pitch-correction plug-in on the market, has no competitors in the RTAS category. In the TMD category, however, there are also the TC Intonator from TC Works and the Pitch Doctor from Wave Mechanics to consider. The Auto-Tune offers the advantage of a graphic mode, but the TC Intonator is sparing of resources and opens two Intonator plug-ins on a single DSP chip.

Special Effects

Needless to say there are a large number of other tools that deliver outstanding special effects or sound processing. In this context, the AudioSuite plug-in VocAlign from Synchro Arts deserves first mention. It was developed to simplify the synchronisation of messy ADR. ADR (automatic dialog replacement) allows film directors to concentrate on the images (rather than the sound) at the time of shooting. The dialogue is lip-synced by the actors later in what is called an ADR booth. The trouble is, some actors are better at this than others, which is where VocAlign comes in. Using a process known as time-stretching, VocAlign allows post-production engineers to make the ADR fit the production audio (recorded during the shoot) and with it, therefore, the pictures. The results are outstanding. Of course, the tool can also be (ab)used for other purposes, such as lip-syncing a choir.

Amp Simulation

Most of the plug-ins in this category are designed to emulate particular guitar amplifiers and speakers, so that a guitarist can lay down a track without having to lug his entire paraphernalia of amps and speakers into the studio with him. There are two contenders: the AmpFarm from Line 6 and the SansAmp from Bomb Factory. On the TDM platform, the AmpFarm is particularly popular with guitarists. The SansAmp only operates in the RTAS environment.

Software Instruments

Now that computers have become far more powerful, software instruments can be implemented easily. The HTDM collection from Native Instruments is particularly to be recommended and includes Battery (a drum sampler), Pro 52 (recreating the Prophet Five from Sequential Circuits) and the B 4 (a virtual B 3 organ). These tone generators are so well integrated into the Pro Tools environment that you can even control their parameters using Pro Tools automation. The Access Virus TDM and Synthesizer One from McDSP, on the other hand, occupy a special place: so far, these are the only software instruments that use the DSPs of a TDM system to do their processing – to the considerable relief of the host CPU! Those tone generators that are integrated into the Pro Tools mixer using DirectConnect – and they include the SoftSampleCell from Digidesign, all further development of which has ceased, all the products of Native Instruments and many others – are integrated less fully than RTAS or HTDM plug-ins, because they are opened as separate applications and cannot therefore benefit from Pro Tools automation.

6 PRO TOOLS AND MIDI

With Version 5.0 of the software, Digidesign converted Pro Tools into a fully functional audio/MIDI workstation that can be used for communication with, and the control of, external MIDI devices as well as software-based synthesisers and samplers. All MIDI data can be edited with precision parallel to the audio tracks in both the Mix and the Edit windows.

MIDI Via OMS

Of course, in its MIDI implementation, Digidesign has adopted a different approach to that of, for example, Logic Audio. Whilst Logic addresses all MIDI devices – even in conjunction with the Digidesign DAE – via user-specific environments (see 'Pro Tools and Emagic Logic'), Pro Tools – whether TDM, LE or Free – is dependent upon Opcode's 'Open Music System' (OMS) – so much so, in fact, that you cannot even start the Pro Tools software unless OMS has first been installed on the computer, whether you intend to use MIDI or not.

Installing OMS

Accordingly, Digidesign has included on the Pro Tools CD ROM a separate installation program for OMS, which you should execute immediately after installing Pro Tools. When you install Pro Tools Free, the OMS installation program is automatically copied to your hard disk.

How Does OMS Function Under Pro Tools?
What Is OMS?

OMS is a set of extensions and programs that bridges the gap between your Pro Tools software and your MIDI hardware. Since in the first instance the OMS cannot

The OMS installation program is on the Pro Tools CD-ROM

tell what MIDI hardware you are working with, one of its key components is a special configuration program (called OMS Setup), which is installed on your computer and helps you create and store a detailed description of all the devices in your current studio in a Studio Setup file, which Pro Tools will read each time it starts up. The result is that whenever you click on the Input or Output buttons on a MIDI track and the pop-up menu opens, you will find all the relevant MIDI devices listed and be able to access them immediately. The principal advantages of all this are, firstly, that you only need to define your MIDI configuration once, and, secondly, that you can access the MIDI devices in your studio as easily as the inputs and outputs of your Pro Tools hardware.

Selecting Ports

When you first run OMS Setup after installation, you will be asked to which of your computer's ports your MIDI hardware is connected, the options listed being

Printer or Modem, since many MIDI interfaces are still designed to comply with the protocols of either or both of these ports. If, however, you are using a USB interface such as Digidesign's MIDI In/Out, you should check neither of these boxes, since the USB port will be interrogated in the course of the following routine and any MIDI interface connected to it will be recognised automatically – provided, that is, you have installed the driver in the OMS (System) folder. Next, as we have mentioned, OMS scans the printer, modem or USB port and identifies the MIDI interface as well as the I/O ports belonging to it. In the final step, you will be invited to define any MIDI devices connected to the ports of your interface that OMS has failed to identify automatically. When you have finished, activate the configuration using the Make Current command in the OMS File menu, and Pro Tools will then adopt this I/O configuration and pass the information on to all parts of the program that relate to MIDI.

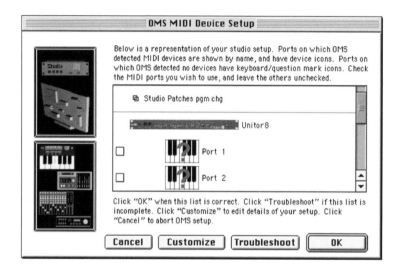

Once OMS has recognised the driver for your interface, its ports are scanned for MIDI devices

Modem Versus Printer

In terms of timing, the modem protocol is considered more stable than the printer protocol, but you may find that you need your modem port to take advantage of Internet, in which case, unless you have a USB interface, you will have no choice but to connect your MIDI hardware to the printer port. USB interfaces, of course, have the advantage of leaving both serial ports free for the purposes for which they were originally intended.

Drivers

As part of the OMS installation, drivers for a large number of popular MIDI interfaces are automatically copied to your computer's system folder. If, however, your interface is not among them, you will have to install the driver yourself before running OMS Setup, as otherwise it will not be recognised.

MIDI Tracks In Pro Tools

Pro Tools processes the MIDI events, displayed as MIDI tracks in the Mix and Edit windows, parallel to the audio data. Unlike audio tracks or aux inputs, however, no audio-specific channel parameters such as inserts or sends (see Chapter 2, 'The Basics') are provided for MIDI tracks. The MIDI ports and devices registered with the OMS during the Setup program are automatically available from the I/O section of each MIDI track. You can enter MIDI data using any device registered as an input device, edit parameters such as Volume and Pan, and transmit the data to the MIDI port of your choice.

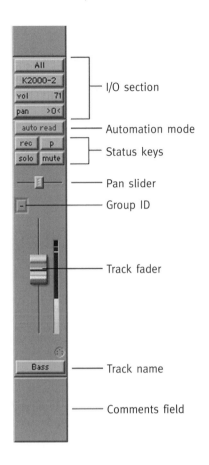

- I/O section
- Automation mode
- Status keys
- Pan slider
- Group ID
- Track fader
- Track name
- Comments field

The Default Program button (marked p) opens the Program Change window. Here you can select a patch or program for the MIDI device you are controlling as well as the sound bank in which it is located.

Audio and MIDI tracks are treated in almost exactly the same way. Not only do their channel strips in the Mix window look much alike but the same principle informs their display in the Edit window. However, whereas in the case of an audio track it is the amplitude of the waveforms that is most commonly displayed along the time axis, with MIDI tracks it is usually the pitch, for which purpose the image of a piano keyboard is displayed on the left of the window with the MIDI events unfolding in chronological order from left to right. The advantage of allowing audio and MIDI tracks to be displayed in parallel is that you can compare the timing of their audio, MIDI and controller data and quickly correct any errors.

To speed the learning process and make the task of recording and editing as intuitive as possible, the designers have gone out of their way to ensure that in terms of tools, techniques and ways of working, MIDI and audio tracks are alike as they could usefully be.

But for the absence of inserts and sends, MIDI tracks resemble audio tracks in the Mix window

The Default Program determines the bank- and program-change messages sent to your MIDI device each time the track plays

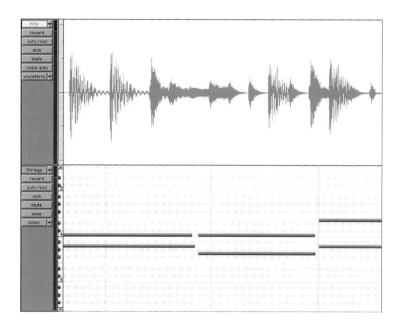

In the Edit window, you can compare audio and MIDI data

MIDI Recording

As we saw in Chapter 3, the procedure for recording an audio track in Pro Tools begins as follows: first you define its physical input and output in the I/O section of the track display ; then you record-enable the track by clicking on the rec button. The procedure for recording MIDI tracks is much the same, though in this case the

I/O section affords you access to the MIDI devices registered with Pro Tools through their definitions in the OMS Studio Setup file. The Input pop-up menu, for example, shows all the MIDI input devices registered with the system. Of course, you can only select as an input device one that has been defined as an input device using the MIDI menu's Input Devices dialog.

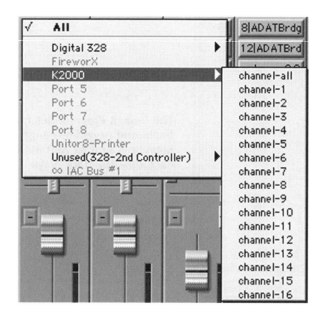

In the Input pop-up menu, you can only select those devices that have been defined as input devices

MIDI Output

On the output side there is no such limitation, though here it must be noted that software synthesisers such as the Virus plug-in from Access cannot be accessed as part of your OMS Studio Setup but form part of the Pro Tools plug-in pool. As a result, you have first to load the plug-in – described in OMS terminology as a 'virtual node' – before you will see it listed in the output pop-up menu of a MIDI track.

MIDI Thru

In the MIDI menu, there is an important item labelled MIDI Thru. MIDI input devices are usually operated with what is termed 'local control' turned off; the keyboard of the input device, in other words, is disconnected from its internal tone generation section; the MIDI messages generated by the keyboard are first processed by Pro Tools and only then transmitted to a MIDI tone generator. Switching off local control prevents the tone generator of the input device, which is not the intended recipient of the messages, sounding at the same time as the intended output device. The MIDI Thru function ensures that the MIDI messages from the keyboard that are being recorded are also relayed to the selected MIDI output. Otherwise even though the routing may be correct and the track meters show that a signal is being received, at the time of recording you will in fact hear nothing.

First Recording

Once you have selected your input and output devices and activated the MIDI Thru function, the first take can proceed in the normal way. How do you proceed if you are basically happy with the take but would like to just go over certain passages again?

MIDI Merge

The simplest way is to perform an overdub as you would with an audio track, but in the case of a MIDI track, you have the choice of either replacing the original material in the selected passages altogether or simply adding to it. In the latter case, you need to switch to MIDI Merge mode, which you can access from the MIDI Controls in the extended Transport window (see 'MIDI Controls'). When the MIDI Merge symbol (which is in the top right hand corner of the Transport window) is illuminated, data added in each subsequent pass is added to the material already present on the track; otherwise each new take simply replaces the one before as is the case with an ordinary overdub.

The MIDI Merge button determines whether the new data is merged with or replaces the old

Editing MIDI Data
Powerful Functions

You may prefer to dispense with further recording and simply edit the material already recorded on the track. As is the case with audio data, switching to the Edit menu allows you to access and modify the recorded material in the track. Various functions are offered to simplify the task of editing.

Quantize

Normally you quantize the starting point of MIDI events by making them snap to the nearest line on a grid. The size of the mesh can be anything from a whole note (semibreve) down to a single tick. A further option is to quantize the end point of notes so that each note is held for its full value, be it a whole note, half note (minim), quarter note (crotchet) or whatever.

Change Duration

Another way of changing the length of a note is offered by the Change Duration function, which offers a number of different approaches to the task. You can, for example, set all note lengths to the same value, increase or reduce them by a set amount or stipulate that they should be lengthened or shortened by a random amount within a chosen range (expressed as a percentage of the original length).

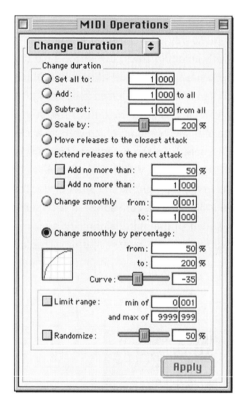

The Change Duration dialog in the MIDI menu offers access to the lengths of the selected MIDI notes

Change Velocity

The Change Velocity function is analogous to Change Duration. In the case of a keyboard, 'velocity' is the measure of how hard a given note was struck. Again, you can give a fixed velocity to all the selected notes, increase or decrease the velocity by a given amount or percentage, or randomise it within a specifiable percentage range.

Change Pitch

The Transpose function allows you to raise or lower the pitch of the selected note or notes by up to 60 semitones.

Whilst these menu functions are primarily designed for the editing of MIDI notes, the Edit Tools in the Edit window and the MIDI Event List in the Windows menu afford access to all MIDI events including controller and SysEx data.

The MIDI Toolkit

You are already familiar with the Toolbar in the Edit window; it was discussed in Chapter 4, 'Editing'. In the case of MIDI data, however, the range of functions of certain tools is slightly different:

- **Zoomer** – The Zoomer performs the same function with MIDI as with audio tracks, serving to increase or decrease the scale of the display.

- **Trimmer** – When editing MIDI notes, the Trimmer fulfils essentially the same role as it does with audio data by lengthening or shortening the selected events. However when the track is displaying controller data, the Trimmer can be used to change the value range (0–127) of the data in question.

- **Selector** – The Selector performs the same function when editing MIDI tracks as audio tracks.

- **The Grabber** – The Grabber can be used to select individual MIDI notes and then move them freely along the x (time) or y (pitch) axes. When a MIDI track is displaying controller data, the Grabber can be used to modify it (within the range 0–127).

- **Scrubber** – The Scrubber cannot be used with MIDI tracks.

- **Pencil** – The Pencil can be used to enter MIDI notes and/or controller data manually. If the MIDI track is displaying controller data, you can use the Pencil to draw values in the range of 0–127.

The MIDI Event List

Whilst the Edit window only offers access to one type of MIDI data at a time (Notes, Velocity, Mute, Pan, Pitch Bend, Program Change and so on), the MIDI Event List, which is accessed from the Windows menu, offers access to all the MIDI events of a track simultaneously.

In some cases, it may be desirable to filter out certain types of event, so that, for example, only pitch bend, velocity values or controller data is shown. The Insert menu affords you an opportunity of adding new MIDI events, such as notes or pitch bend, volume, pan or controller data, to the list.

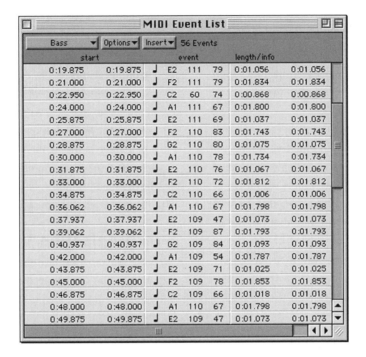

All the MIDI data pertaining to a track is displayed in the MIDI Event List

MIDI Controls

Of course, Pro Tools' MIDI implementation is by no means limited to MIDI tracks. The Ruler Timelines (see Chapter 2, 'The Basics') translate the information in the Tempo

Map into MIDI events that can be exported to any port in your OMS Studio Setup. One way to access the parameters for this function is to select Transport window Shows > MIDI Controls from the Display menu.

The MIDI controls in the Transport window offer access to tempo-related MIDI parameters

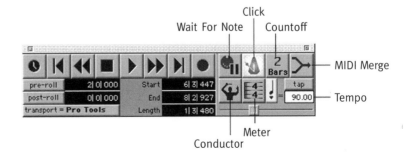

These MIDI controls have the following functions:

- **Wait For Note** – When this button is active, recording does not begin until the first MIDI event has been received.

- **Click** – When this button is active, Pro Tools will generate a MIDI Click during recording and/or playback to serve as a metronome. The same function can be accessed from the MIDI menu via the item Click. To select the port as well as determine the pitch and velocity of the click, open the Click Options dialog in the MIDI menu.

- **Countoff** – When this button is active, Pro Tools will give you your cue so you don't miss your entry; it does this by playing back a specifiable amount of the passage prior to the one you are about to re-record. If you so desire, you can also hear a specifiable amount of the passage that follows it.

- **MIDI Merge** – When this function is active, newly recorded MIDI data is merged with the existing events on a MIDI track. Otherwise the new data simply overwrites the old.

- **Conductor** – When the Conductor is selected, the Tempo Map defined by the Tempo Ruler controls the speed of recording and/or playback. When it is deselected, Pro Tools switches to Manual Mode.

- **Tempo** – In Manual Mode, you can enter a new tempo by typing in a new value in beats per minute (BPM), by tapping whilst the Tempo field is selected, or by moving the tempo slider in the Transport window.

- **Meter** – The Meter button displays the current time signature, that is to say, the one that is active at the current cursor location. Whenever the time signature of the music changes, you simply insert a new Meter Event in the Meter Track. You can do this by entering a new value in the Tempo/Meter Change window that appears when you double-click the Meter button in the Transport window or when you select the item Change Meter from the MIDI menu.

Synchronisation Via MIDI

Further options relating to Pro Tools' MIDI implementation can be accessed from the Peripherals dialog in the Setups menu. Each of the register cards Synchronisation, Machine Control and MIDI Controllers

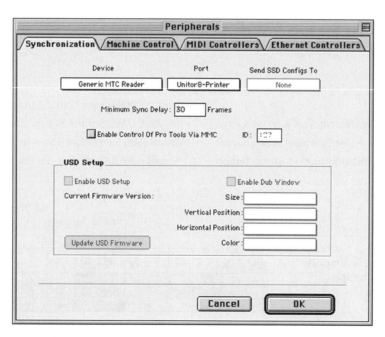

The Peripherals dialog controls the communication between Pro Tools and external controllers and/or tape recorders

lists parameters relating to a different aspect of the communication with external tape decks, video recorders, mixing consoles and hardware controllers.

SMPTE

The Synchronisation register card offers a way of synchronising Pro Tools with external, Capable-capable devices. Normally the synchronisation between AV devices is implemented using the SMPTE protocol, in which the absolute playback position is measured in Hours, Minutes, Seconds, Frames and Sub-Frames. The hardware synchronisers Universal Slave Driver (Pro Tools Mix) or Sync I/O (Pro Tools HD systems), configured in the bottom half of the register card, provide a bridge between Pro Tools and professional video or tape recorders.

MTC

Under other circumstances, you may wish to operate Pro Tools in harness with an external sequencer or record the automation data of a digital mixing console. MIDI Time Code (MTC), which is similar to SMPTE and supported by a large number of devices, is provided for this type of application. With MTC, no external synchroniser is necessary as the MIDI interface usurps its role to a large extent.

Slave

If you want Pro Tools to operate as a slave to an external device, activate the option Generic MTC Reader from the Device pop-up menu and select the device in your OMS studio that you wish to assume the role of clock master. It is advisable to select Enable Control of Pro Tools via MMC. This will give the external device the ability to control Pro Tools' transport functions.

Master

You could also operate Pro Tools as MTC master. To do this, open the next register card, Machine Control, and activate MIDI Machine Code by selecting Enable. Using the Send To pop-up, select the MIDI device that you wish to trigger using the transport functions of Pro Tools. For synchronisation to be possible, Pro Tools must transmit MIDI Machine Code to the external device. To get it to do this, you have to open the Session Setup window (Windows › Show Session Setup), activate the MTC to Port box in the Generate Time Code dialog and select the requisite OMS output in the associated pop-up menu. You can also adjust the MTC output using the pop-ups Frame Rate (format: 24, 25, 29.97, 29.97 drop, 30, 30 drop) and Session Start (Hours: Minutes: Seconds: Frames).

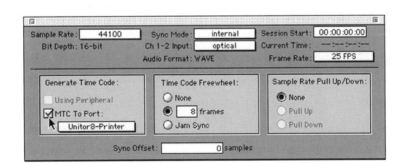

The Session Setup window is used to set the MIDI Time Code parameters

Generic MTC

If you activate MIDI Machine Control whilst synchronisation is being controlled by the Generic MTC Reader, Pro Tools will run as a slave to the external MIDI device. The transport functions, of course, are controlled by the Pro Tools Transport window.

MIDI Beat Clock

If you're in the situation where you need to synchronise older drum computers, hardware sequencers or arpeggiators with Pro Tools, this is possible to achieve by selecting the option MIDI Beat Clock located in the MIDI menu.

MIDI Controllers

The two remaining register cards in the Peripherals dialog are used for the configuration off external hardware controllers. Pro Control and Control 24 are control surfaces specially designed by Digidesign for the control of Pro Tools. They communicate with the computer via Ethernet and are therefore configured using the fourth register card, Ethernet Controllers.

Various other manufacturers offer more affordable options for the control of Pro Tools. The least powerful offer remote control of Pro Tools' transport keys and faders and little more, but Mackie's HUI can even control a number of plug-ins in Pro Tools tracks and display track levels on an integrated meter bridge. Up to four such controllers can be used at once. They are configured using the MIDI Controllers register card.

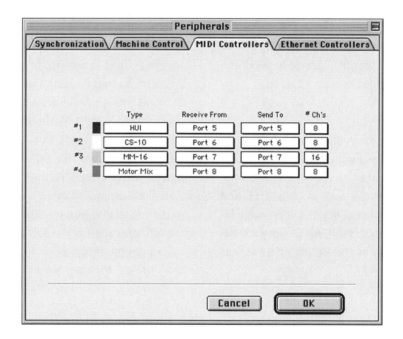

In the MIDI Controllers register card, you can configure up to four external hardware controllers

Presets And Ports

Via the Type pop-up menu, you can choose between seven different controller presets that were stored in the Controllers folder (System > DAE > Controllers) during the installation. Next select the inputs and outputs through which the controller will communicate with the Pro Tools software. Using the pop-up menus Receive From and Send To select the ports through which the hardware controller is registered in the OMS Studio Setup. Finally register the MIDI controller for the input of MIDI data into Pro Tools via the Input Devices dialog in the MIDI menu.

Colour-Indicated Remote Control

If you close the dialog box and switch to the Mix or Edit window, you will see that the track names are now framed with coloured lines. This indicates that these tracks are now being controlled by the hardware controller currently selected. Some hardware controllers can control eight tracks, others 16 tracks, the first eight (or 16) tracks being assigned to the first controller on the list, the next eight (or 16) tracks to the second listed, and so on. The maximum number of tracks that can be assigned to MIDI controllers in Pro Tools is 64.

Reordering Tracks

A given track's controller assignment is based simply upon its position in the Mix and Edit windows. Changing the order of each individual track will therefore have the effect of altering its controller assignments, and you can ensure that a controller will be assigned to a hitherto unassigned track simply by moving it nearer the top of the Edit window, which has the same effect as moving it further to the left of the Mix window.

7 MIXING

Mixdown

The mixdown is the culmination of all the work of recording, monitoring, editing and processing with plug-ins that has gone before. The task is to examine the materials at hand, make comparisons – modifications, if need be – harmonise, polish, adapt, until an artistically satisfying and technically flawless mix emerges, in a format that will ensure its smooth integration into the mastering process.

Rough Mix

In practice, the task of mixing begins at the recording stage, because you need to create at least a rough mix before you can even think about making a satisfactory acoustic assessment of the audio events. The top priority here is to ensure that all the sound sources in the session can be heard clearly. That in itself isn't too difficult, since there is a volume fader in the Mix window for every track. Unlike audio tracks, however, MIDI tracks emit only messages, the actual sound being produced as a rule by an external device that is initially not part of the Pro Tools mix. Now may also be the time to add an output fader to the end of the signal chain to control the sum of all the audio signals and determine the output format of the mix file. In other words, the setup of your session will need further refinement before you can embark on a final mixdown.

Routing
Output Routing

At the beginning of the session, you created audio and MIDI tracks into which regions were inserted in the course of recording and these were later edited.

The relative level of the audio tracks is determined by the track faders and the results sent to the output you selected as the Default Output in the I/O Setup dialog accessed from the Setup menu. In most cases, this will be one of the mono or stereo outputs of your interface, but using the Output register card, you can also define a multi-channel output, which will allow you to output your mix in surround format. At the moment, however, you have no way either of independently controlling the level of your output or of processing its signals using plug-ins. It is therefore advisable to create a master fader using the New Track command in the File menu. A choice of output formats ranging from mono to 7.1 is offered and you can now control the output level of the audio sum using the track fader. You can also load effects plug-ins to the insert section of the master fader to apply compression to the sum, perhaps, or equalisation or to control the output level with a loudness maximiser. It should be noted that in master fader tracks, any plug-ins are switched post-fader.

Live Inputs

Your session also contains MIDI tracks that transmit messages used to control external MIDI tone generators or software synthesisers. Where you are using external MIDI devices, the problem arises that the output of the track obviously cannot be routed to Pro Tools' audio sum directly because all it consists of is control messages and not audio data. What you need to do, then, is connect your external tone generators to Pro Tools, so that their output can be mixed with that of the audio tracks. This is done by creating the requisite number of auxiliary inputs using the New Track command in the File menu. In the Input section of the new track or tracks, select the hardware inputs to which your MIDI tone generators are connected. The aux input will now function as a live input, with its level controlled by the track fader, its position in the stereo image by the panorama slider, and its data processed (if need be) by plug-ins. As a result, the MIDI instrument will be present in the main mix along with all the audio tracks and controlled by the master fader. The same procedure, incidentally, is recommended for software instruments. Admittedly you could, if you wanted to, use them as plug-ins in ordinary audio tracks, but then they would take up

at least one Pro Tools voice, which as aux inputs they do not.

Effects Returns

Aux inputs can also be used as effects returns. As we saw in Chapter 5, 'Plug-ins', reverberation, delay and even modulation effects can be introduced into the mix via the auxiliary sends in the audio channel strips. The aux sends feed internal busses that in turn feed the inputs of the auxiliary input channel containing the plug-in. The fader of the aux input channel then controls the level of processed signal added to the main mix along with the other instruments.

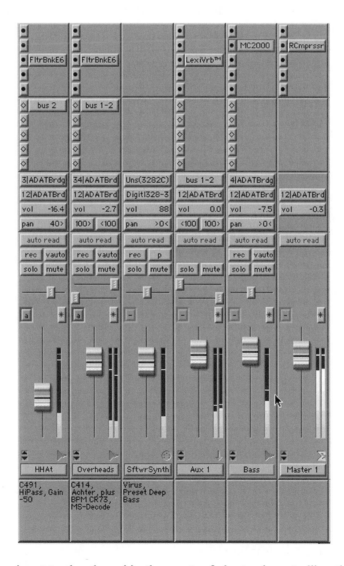

Audio, MIDI and auxiliary input tracks alongside the master fader track controlling the sum

Session-Routing Checklist

1 Create a master fader so that you can control the level of, and apply plug-in processors to, the main audio mix

2 Create aux inputs for use as live inputs for external MIDI tone generators

3 Create additional aux inputs to serve as effects returns for the aux system of your Pro Tools mixer

4 Route all tracks to your master fader

5 For each shared effect, define a global aux send in all tracks. Route all aux sends intended for the same effect to the same DAE buss and feed it into an aux input channel. Load the relevant plug-in to the insert section of the aux input channel.

Group Functions And The Creation Of Submixes
Creating Groups

In Chapter 2, 'The Basics', we saw how any number of tracks could combine to form mix and/or edit groups. By creating a mix group comprising all the channels derived from a single sound source, such as a drum set captured by multiple microphones, or a group of instruments sharing the same function (such as all the rhythm guitars), you can work far more efficiently. Grouping affects the following channel functions:

• Volume
• Solo
• Mute
• Automation mode
• Send level
• Send mutes
• Track view
• Track height
• Edit functions (provided it is an Edit and Mix group)

If you change the status of any of these parameters in any track within the group, all the tracks in the group are similarly affected but without disturbing their levels relative to each other; that is to say the level of all group members is raised or lowered by the same amount and any differences between group members is therefore retained.

Grouping Functions In Mixing

By the same token, muting one channel in a group mutes the entire group, and changes in the send level or send mute status of one group member affect all group members alike, with the relationship between group members again remaining unchanged (provided that you have selected the options Send Mutes Follow Groups and Send Levels Follow Group in the Setups › Preferences › Automation register card). Digidesign has wisely opted not to include functions such as panning, either of the track or of the sends, and output routing among the group functions, so you can still pan each track individually and assign it to a separate output.

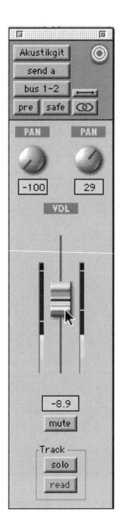

The pan controllers in the sends section are not subject to group control

Audio Submixes

An even simpler procedure is to create an audio submix comprising the signals of multiple tracks. Here the output of the selected tracks is routed via a DAE buss (whether mono, stereo or multi-channel) to an aux input instead of the main mix. The aux input now operates as a sub master, the output of which is added to the main sum. With this routing arrangement, it remains possible to adjust the level, panning and muting of each track individually and feed its signal independently to an internal send buss. Changing the parameters of the aux input channel, however, is equivalent aurally to making the same parameter changes to each of its component tracks.

Advantages And Disadvantages Of Mix Groups…

Which of the two procedures is more efficient depends on the circumstances. The drawback of using mix groups is that plug-ins have to be loaded individually for each track, whereas with a submix you only need to load the plug-in once (into the insert of the aux input track) and it will process the sum of all the tracks in the submix. Soloing, however, is far less problematic with mix groups than submixes. You can solo a mix group by soloing any of its members. When you try to solo a submix, on the other hand, what you get is silence, because soloing the submix has the unfortunate side-effect of muting the tracks being fed into it.

…And Submixes

One way round the problem is to define a mix group that includes both the submix and its component tracks, in which case soloing the submix does not mute the tracks being fed into it, but this creates a problem when you try to adjust the relative levels of the tracks in the submix, as they are now grouped and changing the level of one changes that of them all. The submix principle also produces a slight, though on occasion problematic degree of latency, which in the case of multi-miked sound sources can cause phasing problems and even acoustic cancellation. As you can see, before deciding whether to opt for a group or submix channel configuration, you need to

give a little thought to the question of which operations you are likely to perform most frequently as well as to the musical content.

The Mix
Minimum Requirements

As we have already mentioned, the least you can ask of a mix is that it should make it possible to hear all the sonic events. That's the compulsory programme, if you like, and the free programme is all that smacks of artistry and makes for a high quality, professional mix. In both endeavours, Pro Tools gives you every chance of success.

Getting Started

The first phase of the mixing process always follows the same pattern: you set the signal levels for each track using the track fader and then position it in the stereo image using the panorama slider. The next step is to listen carefully to each track in turn and decide what signal processing (if any) is required to improve it. The inserts section can accommodate up to five plug-ins per track, though as a rule you will not need that many (or else will be unable to load them on account of limited processing capacity).

EQ

Loading one equaliser per track to modify the frequency spectrum certainly makes sense. Along with volume and pan, EQ that is flawless from both an artistic and a technical point of view has the effect of adding depth and clarity to the mix.

Dynamics

Drums and vocals certainly also profit from compression, which serves to optimise the dynamics of the mix.

Additional Plug-ins

If the resources of the system permit, you can experiment with additional plug-ins; effects such as an Expander/Gate remove noise from the mix and improve the overall transparency, whilst psychoacoustic equalisers or harmonisers can enhance tracks from both an acoustic and a harmonic standpoint.

Reverb And Delay

Regardless of how many plug-ins you want to lavish upon individual tracks, be sure to allow sufficient processing capacity for reverb, delay and summing plug-ins. Effects like reverb and delay provide good spatial imaging and are generally indispensable. These effects are accessed via the track sends (therefore over the DAE buss system) and reintroduced into the mix via the aux inputs. All of this involves additional overheads in terms of timeslot usage and claims on the capacity of the DSPs or host CPU.

Sum Effects

It is also advisable to allow for effects such as a compressor, an EQ or a maximiser in the main mix.

By loading these sum effects into the inserts section of the master fader, you will be able whilst mixing in order to perform tasks such as sum compression and limiting that would otherwise require a separate mastering process.

System Overheads

The Show System Usage command in the Windows menu allows you to see how much processing capacity is currently available in your computer's operating system. If capacity is running a little low, one possible solution is to dispense for the time being with the sum effects, postponing the performance of the corresponding tasks until the mastering stage.

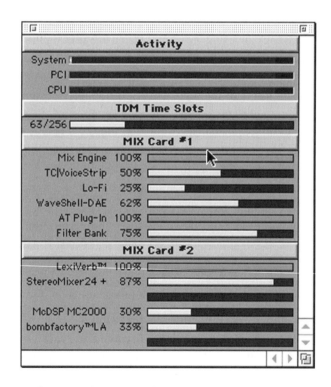

This window indicates how much processing power is still available in your system

Mixing Checklist

1 Check the routing of all tracks. all tracks other than MIDI tracks should be routed to the master fader of your session.

2 Using the track faders and pan sliders, create a general rough mix by setting the levels of the individual tracks and their position within the main mix.

3   Plan your plug-in assignments. Be sure to leave sufficient processing power for effects like reverb and delay. If need be, individual tracks can be processed by RTAS plug-ins or destructively via AudioSuite.

4   Load the plug-ins into your audio tracks, aux inputs and master fader.

5   Assign suitable busses (mono, stereo or multi-channel) to the aux sends. Connect your aux inputs to the appropriate DAE buses.

6   Check the sound of each individual instrument and if need be adjust the parameters of its plug-ins (EQ, dynamics processors and so on).

7   Listen again to your rough mix. If need be, readjust the volume ratios. Under some circumstances it may be a good idea to introduce effects at this stage and then further readjust the individual channels in the light of the changes.

8   Set the aux send levels using the send faders in each channel. If your routing is correct, you will be able to check the level of the aux inputs receiving the signal optically. You should also be able to hear each effect, provided the aux input fader is set sufficiently high. Check the wet/dry mix control to ensure that only the processed (wet) signal is being output, as the dry signal emitted by the plug-in will be out of phase with the identical signal in the output of the source audio track.

9   If you are working with stereo sends, check that their panning accords with that of the track output. As a rule, wet and dry signals from the same source should occupy the same position in the stereo image.

10 Now adjust the level of the effects returns and aux inputs in relation to that of the other tracks. Make sure that the signals are not out of phase with each other.

Metering

Your rough mix should now be sounding considerably better than when you began. This is often a good moment to switch to post-fader metering in your audio tracks. All the time you were recording, editing and applying plug-in processors to the audio tracks, it made sense to use the Pre-Fader Metering option in the Operations menu, so that you could pick up on any overload distortion in the signal chain (introduced by a plug-in perhaps). Now that you have optimised the individual tracks, you can afford to deactivate this option, so that the meters again take account of the position of the track faders. This will allow you to monitor the volume ratios of different tracks visually.

Automation

With all this, we have still far from exhausted the possibilities, since with internal automation, Pro Tools offers a feature that, as recently as a few years ago, was reserved for high-end studios and even there was only available for a limited number of parameters. Pro Tools, in contrast, permits the automation of all track parameters relevant to mixing, including those of plug-ins. When this automation is combined with the use of an external hardware controller, such as the Control24 (TDM systems) or the Digi002 (Pro Tools LE), the work is streamlined still further, as this allows you to enter parameter changes using faders and rotary controls as though you were using an analogue mixer. Even if you have no controller, however, you can still automate even the tiniest details of the mix. Entering the data with the mouse is more laborious, of course, than using faders and potentiometers, but the degree of automation that results in the same in both cases.

Automation Preferences

Automation data also makes demands upon the processing and storage capacity of your computer, even if the demands are rather modest. In the Automation dialog in the Preferences dialog (accessed via the Setups menu), you can specify the amount of memory to reserve for automation recording as well as configuring various other options relating to the display and coupling of automation parameters. An important factor is the Degree of Thinning, which calls for a brief explanation. Depending upon which method you use to control the interface, you may find yourself generating a great deal of redundant data that clogs up your automation buffer. By selecting Thin Automation in the Edit window, you can prevent this happening. In the section Degree of Thinning, you can choose between None, Little, Some, More and Most. Here you must take care not to throw out the baby with the bathwater: you do not wish to simplify to the point of distortion, which can happen when you select Most; the Some option, on the other hand, represents a good compromise, eliminating some of the detail without subverting your intentions.

The Automation tab of the Preferences dialog used to configure the automation parameters

Automation Using A Mixing Controller

In the MIDI chapter, we touched upon the subject of MIDI control surfaces. These are hardware mixing units with faders and rotary controls that allow you to control the parameters in the Pro Tools mixer manually via MIDI. First you must first register the hardware with Pro Tools (Setups > Peripherals > MIDI Controller) and thereafter you will be able to control the faders, pan sliders and even the parameters of your plug-ins with both hands, as though you were using a hardware mixer, instead of having to rely upon the keyboard and the mouse. The bandwidth of MIDI is, of course, comparatively limited: due to the MIDI specification, the control range of a conventional controller (and therefore also of any Pro Tools parameters controlled by it) is limited to 128 discrete steps (because there are only seven bits), whereas Pro Tools operates internally at a resolution of up to 16.7 million steps (24 bits). On the face of it, therefore, a fade-out created using a MIDI control surface is never going to be even remotely as smooth as one that Pro Tools could create if left to its own devices. But there are MIDI controllers and MIDI controllers. Through the adoption of a 'smart MIDI' approach, the HUI from Mackie and its emulation by Logic Control are capable of attaining the same resolution as Digidesign's own controllers.

Digidesign Controllers

Very good results can be achieved with the Digidesign controllers, Control|24 and Pro Control, which are installed via the Ethernet Controllers register card (Setups › Peripherals). Both devices operate using a parameter resolution of 10 bits, which yields 1,024 discrete steps. This value is, however, intelligently interpolated by the software so that parameter changes can in fact be implemented in 24-bit resolution, which is optimal. And this resolution is available for all parameters, whether fader, pan or plug-in – provided, of course, the plug-in itself operates in 24-bit resolution, which some do not.

Colour Coding

In practice, the automation is relatively simple to set up. Once you have registered your mixing control surface with Pro Tools via the Peripherals dialog, Pro Tools tracks are framed by coloured boxes. The colour coding indicates the relation between hardware control elements and the software controls. If you move a hardware fader, for example, the corresponding onscreen fader will follow the movement. The same goes for the hardware rotary controls to which functions such as panning, the control of aux sends or the adjustment of plug-in parameters can be assigned. Of course, these movements will not, without more, affect your mix, since your work has to be protected against the inadvertent nudging of faders. first then, you have to configure the automation of the track or tracks to which the control surface is to be assigned.

Automation Setup And Modes
Total Recall

Even though the overall framework of your mix may be good, there may still be individual parameters that require adjustment. It is not necessary to automate all the channel settings in the mixer, as your basic settings will in any case be reloaded each time you open the session due to Pro Tools' 'total recall' principle of operation. You should therefore only automate those parameters that really require it, leaving the others to be reloaded and stored from the session file. These parameters are the faders, perhaps the pan and some of the parameters of the mixers, since you are unlikely

to want to change any of the other parameters in real-time. What is needed, therefore, is a selective automation that concentrates on certain parameters and ignores the rest.

Parameter Selection

This approach is implemented in Pro Tools via the Show Automation Enable item in the Windows menu. In the Automation Enable window, you can select which of the following parameters you wish to automate:

*   Volume
*   Pan
*   Mute
*   Plug-in
*   Send level
*   Send pan
*   Send mute

Entries that are not highlighted are excluded from automation. You can also specify whether you wish the automation data to act upon the entire file, only the data following the current cursor position or only the data preceding it.

In the Automation Enable window, you select globally the parameters to be automated

Automation Mode

The next step is to set the automation mode in the desired tracks. Normally all the track in the session are set to Auto Read, which means the automation data on the track is read and transferred to the parameters in the track. If you have not yet created any automation data, the track parameters will be those you set during the rough mix. In order to write automation data, you need to change the automation mode using the button in the channel strip and begin playing back the session. Here's a list of the options that are available:

- **Auto Off** – Nothing happens; the automation data is not processed.

- **Auto Write** – In this mode, all the existing automation data is overwritten with the current values. When playback stops, the parameter is reset to its original value and Pro Tools switches the track to Auto Touch mode.

- **Auto Touch** – In this mode, the existing automation data is only overwritten if you actually enter new values (eg by moving a fader). Otherwise, the data is retained. When you release the input controller, the parameter returns to its original value.

- **Auto Latch** – This mode is like Auto Touch except that the writing of automation continues until you stop playback.

- **Trim (TDM only)** – Trim is an extension of the above-mentioned modes and relates exclusively to track faders and send levels. In Trim mode, movement of the fader creates relative values not absolute ones, that is to say, the existing automation data is not overwritten but merely modified by the amount of increase or decrease indicated by the faders. Trim combines with the other automation modes as follows:

    - **Trim + Auto Read** – Trim moves are played back but not written into the automation data. (Useful for trying things out).

- **Trim + Auto Write** – The trim values are applied to the existing automation data

- **Trim + Auto Touch** – When the fader is released, trimming stops and the fader goes back to following the existing automation

- **Trim + Auto Latch** – Once trimming begins, all fader moves increase or decrease the existing automation values until playback stops.

The Automaton mode pop-up menu

Plug-in Automation

Depending upon the mode selected, you can now perfect your rough mix by performing and recording the desired fader and slider movements to control the volume and panning as well as selected plug-in parameters, if you wish. For the automation of plug-ins, you need first to select the plug-in parameters you wish to automate. You do this by opening the window of the plug-in in question and clicking on the auto button in the top panel of the window: in the dialog box that opens, select from the list on the left the parameters you wish to automate and click the Add button to add them to the list on the right hand side. All the parameters thus selected will now be framed either in red (Auto Write, -Touch, -Latch) or green (Auto Read) in the plug-in window and can then be manipulated using the controllers of your hardware control surface and automated by the software. Should you make a mistake, you can always return to the previous automation run by selecting Undo from the Edit menu. If subsequently you decide you want to keep the take after all, select Redo from the same menu.

Automation Using The Pencil

Naturally automation data can also be displayed and edited graphically in the Edit window. It takes the form of a line graph with editable breakpoints, these being the places where the line changes direction, even if only slightly. A separate automation playlist is assigned to each of the parameters capable of being automated (Volume, Pan, Mute) as well as any plug-in parameters you have selected. Click on Track View and select from the pop-up menu the playlist you wish to see. If you select the option Volume, you will see a graph of the fader movements superimposed on the waveform display. In this mode, you cannot access the region underneath; it is simply there as an aid to orientation, but you can edit the automation data itself either by redrawing lines with the Pencil or by moving breakpoints vertically or horizontally at will with the Grabber. In this manner, you can correct, perfect and even delete the automation data you created using your hardware control surface.

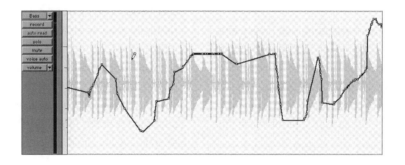

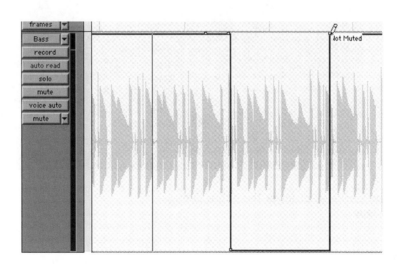

Depending upon the level selected, automation playlists for Volume (top), Muting (bottom) or any other parameter are superimposed on the waveform

Mouse Input

If you cannot afford a hardware controller, you can always use the mouse. Obviously this is a great deal more laborious than using a controller, as you can only regulate one parameter at a time, but the results are essentially no different to those achieved using a hardware control surface. To add automation data, it is sufficient to select the desired automation playlist in the Edit window and enter the control data into the playlist using the Pencil. The automation mode is irrelevant to this type of automation and should therefore be set to Auto Read, as otherwise your automation data could either be truncated, overwritten or corrupted if new controller data were entered inadvertently (for instance from an external MIDI device or a MIDI track).

Pencil Tool

The Pencil allows you to enter automation movements or breakpoints into any automation playlist with almost sample accuracy. As already mentioned, the waveform of the track that is being edited is displayed beneath the automation data, which makes it easy to identify the acoustic events the automation data of which you wish to modify.

Deleting And Modifying Automation Data

Suppose you have automated the Volume in a track but wish to delete part of the automation or even a given breakpoint. Nothing could be easier. All you do is hold down the Option (Mac) or Alt (Windows) key and delete the breakpoint with the Pencil. To delete a passage, select it using the Selector tool and press the Delete key. All the breakpoints will be deleted and Pro Tools will create a continuous line of data between the breakpoints lying immediately to the left and right of the passage deleted. What if the automation within the track is fine but in context with the other tracks altogether too quiet or too loud? No problem. Select a breakpoint in the region with the Trimmer and move the entire automation along the vertical axis to make the entire track louder or softer.

Copying Sequences

Naturally you can also copy a sequence of automation data (by selecting the data in question followed by Copy in the Edit menu) and paste it in the normal way (select the destination followed by Paste in the Edit menu). There are virtually no limits to the editing possibilities in Pro Tools and the results are far superior to anything you could achieve by 'analogue' automation.

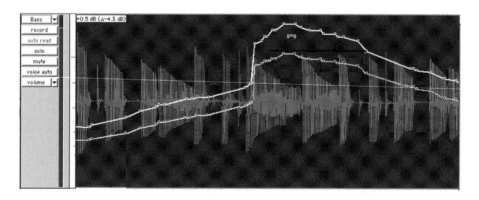

Using the Trimmer you can raise or lower the entire line without altering its shape

Outputting The Mix

When you have optimised your mix by means of the automation, you naturally need to copy it to a mastering medium. One solution is to output the entire mix to a DAT, MI or CD recorder connected to the output to which your master fader is assigned, but this procedure has now largely been superseded in practice.

Bouncing To A Master File

The simpler option is to bounce the entire mix to disk to create a master but without leaving Pro Tools. You can do this by selecting Bounce to Disk from the File menu. This will open the Bounce dialog, giving you the option to select:

- The bounce source (in this case the output of the master fader)

- The file type (SDII, AIFF, WAV, QuickTime, Sound Resource or – if you have installed the necessary codecs – RealAudio or MPEG-1 Layer 3 [also known as MP3])

- The format (Mono Summed, Multiple Mono, Stereo Interleaved or – if defined – Multi-Channel)

- The resolution (8-, 16- or 24-bit)

- The sample rate (42,336kHz–50,000kHz) of the master file

Subsequent Mastering

You can choose whether the conversion to the desired format should be performed during or after the bounce process. For subsequent mastering within Pro Tools, you should select Import After Bounce. When you select Bounce, you must select a storage path. Your mix will now be recorded to the hard disk in real time complete with all the live inputs, plug-ins and automation.

The Bounce Function

Naturally you can now deliver this bounce or master file to an external mastering studio that will handle the further processing and pressing, but you might prefer to perform the job of mastering yourself. After all, apart from a burning program, Pro Tools offers all the functions you need for the mastering process.

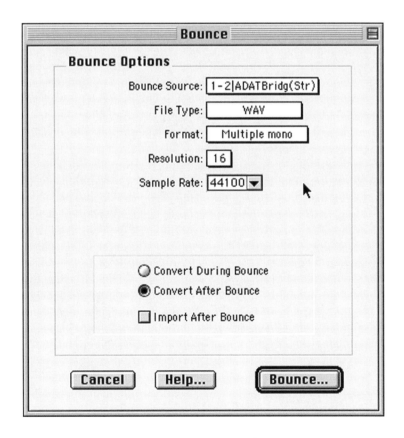

The Bounce dialog sets the parameters for outputting your mix

Burning A CD

Even the burning program is available for separate purchase. Digidesign's MasterList 2.4 is a professional authoring application for Red-Book standard (and therefore glass master capable) audio CDs. All the functions needed for the actual mastering that were described in Chapter 4, 'Editing', and in the preceding sections are available. So you can import the bounced master file directly into Pro Tools as one (stereo) or several (multi-channel) tracks, modify it using the Edit tools and optimise it using plug-ins (AudioSuite, RTAS or TDM). Finally, using the Bounce-to-Disk function described above, you can create the finished file from which MasterList or an application like it will be able to create a Red Book standard CD master that a duplication facility can use as the direct source for glass mastering.

8 PRO TOOLS AND VIDEO

'Digidesign – a division of Avid'. The apposition here not only describes the genealogy of Digidesign but also represents a commitment, since, as a subsidiary of the market leader in the field of digital media technology, Digidesign is heir to certain expectations, one of which is to ensure that their Pro Tools package occupies a position within the industry comparable in importance to that occupied by the digital film and video production systems produced by Avid Technology.

In 1989, Avid introduced the non-linear editing system Media Composer, which blazed the way for today's fully digital film, video and broadcasting industry. Among the most famous Avid systems are not only Media Composer but also Symphony, Film Composer, Avid|DS, Avid Xpress DV and Avid NewsCutter and these cover the entire spectrum of digital film, TV and video production.

Unity, as the say, breeds strength, and since the takeover of Digidesign in 1995 by Avid, the two firms have dominated almost all areas of modern media sound production. Blockbusters such as *Shrek*, *Pearl Harbor* and *Star Wars* could hardly have been realized without the products designed by the Avid group, which is why the producers of these groundbreaking films were more than happy to acknowledge the group's contribution in the closing credits of their work. In addition to the Technical Grammy in 2001, Digidesign and Avid 2001 also picked up two Oscars, if only indirectly: *Black Hawk Down* won in the category Best Film Editing with Avid and Best Sound with Digidesign.

The basis of this success is the intensive collaboration that ensures that core functions are available to both systems. So each Avid System is in principle capable of processing audio data and Pro Tools in its basic version (Macintosh) is capable of importing QuickTime movies. Despite this, the functionality of each in the domain of the other has deliberately been limited, and the strict separation of high end video and high end audio maintained, so as to avoid flooding either system with an unmanageable number of functions.

Importing QuickTime
Video And Multimedia

Without the ability to integrate digital film material into the audio editor, it would be impossible from within Pro Tools to add sound to video clips and multimedia presentations. Digidesign opted for Apple's QuickTime format, which has become the standard for digital video and streaming on the Internet, for the image functions in Pro Tools. As well as being widely distributed, QuickTime had the advantage of being in principle a purely software process that therefore required no additional hardware. For this reason, Pro Tools on its own does not offer any way of capturing QuickTime films (see below under 'The AVoption|XL'). Instead, an import function is provided to allow you to integrate QuickTime movies into your Pro Tools session. Playback is limited to a single video stream so it is not possible to create more than one QuickTime video per session or edit two or more such files simultaneously. In order to create the QuickTime movie, you therefore have to rely upon an external software application and then load the finished clip into Pro Tools.

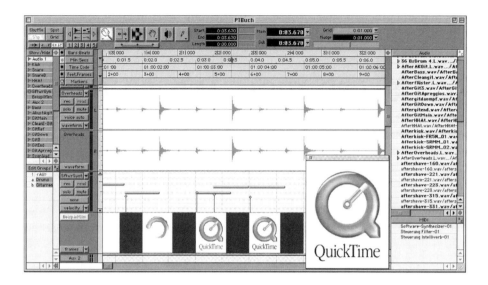

Once imported, the video data is displayed as frames or a block in the video track and played back in the floating Movie window

High Overheads

Depending upon the resolution and the frame rate, QuickTime movies impose a heavy burden upon the computer and peripherals. When Pro Tools is running at the same time, these demands are increased still further, since now not only video but also audio data has to be edited. Depending upon the size of the project, it may sometimes be advisable therefore to access audio and video data from separate data busses and hard drives. Using the Disk Allocation function we looked at in Chapter 3, 'Recording With Pro Tools', you should therefore ensure that the audio data is saved on a hard disk reserved for audio and the video material on a different drive – if possible on a different SCSI buss.

Video Playback Options

The options Medium Priority Playback and Highest Priority Playback in the Movie menu are designed to improve the playback performance over that of the default setting, Normal Priority Playback, however they do so at the expense of other graphic tasks such as the display of Pro Tools meters or fader movements. A different approach is to use a video capture card specially designed for the output of QuickTime data. You will find information about suitable products in the compatibility lists on the Digidesign web site (www.digidesign.com).

Time Code

Another important theme relating to the editing of video data is Pro Tools' time code synchronisation. The playback speed of video data – regardless of whether we are talking about QuickTime or some other video format – occurs at certain predefined frame rates laid down by the Society of Motion Picture and Television Engineers (SMPTE) to standardise the synchronisation of analogue video and sound recording equipment. The playback speed is measured in frames per second (fps).

The frame rate of the Pro Tools session therefore has to be matched to that of the QuickTime video. Select Show Session Setup from the Window menu and select the session's frame rate from the pop-up menu. If you don't do this, the synchronisation of the video with your

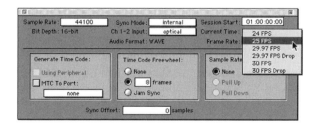

The Session Setup window allows you to set the SMPTE frame rate for the session

audio data may break down on other systems or during subsequent mixing with the original video.

The Import Function

Once you have checked the time code parameters of the session to make sure they match those of the movie in question, select Import Movie from the Movie menu.

Using the Import Movie dialog window, locate and select the QuickTime movie you wish to load, enable the Show Preview check box if you wish to see the first frame, and click Open to import the movie. Now Pro Tools will import the movie and display it in its own video track in the Edit window, whilst displaying the first frame of the movie in a separate floating Movie window.

The Import Movie dialog

QuickTime And Audio

Under some circumstances, the QuickTime film may already contain a mono or stereo audio track that needs to be retained or edited. This audio track is not, however, automatically imported along with the video. If you wish to import it, select Import Audio From Current Movie from the Movie menu. In the dialog box that opens, all the available QuickTime files will be displayed. Select the desired track and confirm with OK. A new dialog box will appear inviting you to select the storage path for this audio file. Once the file has been imported, the audio file will appear in the Audio Regions list in the Edit window, whence it can be dragged to the playlist of the track or tracks of your choice. Needless to say, you will want to synchronise the start of the audio region with the first frame of your movie. The command Import Audio From Other Movie can be used to import additional audio files such as a CD title or the audio data from other video files.

Movie Offset And The Bounce Function

In principle, the first frame of a video sequence is always synchronised with the start of your session.

The clip is automatically inserted at the start of the playlist and cannot be manually shifted along the time axis. Pro Tools does, however, offer another way of fine-tuning the start point of your movie. Select Set Movie Offset from the Movie menu and enter the desired offset value in quarter frames, the maximum offset being ±120 quarter frames.

The correct way to proceed is to synchronise the audio regions of your session with the images. In the Edit window, enable Grid mode (see Chapter 4, 'Editing') and set the grid resolution to frames by selecting Frames in the Nudge/Grid pop-up menu. Using the Selector, create a sync point within the movie track. Now when you drag an audio file from the Audio Regions list whilst holding down the Control key, the starting point of the region will automatically snap to the sync point in the movie track. Using the same system, you can now insert all the audio data for your movie track into the right places for inclusion in the mix.

Exporting The Film

When you have finished mixing, you will want to create a new QuickTime movie with the new soundtrack. Select Bounce To Movie from the Movie menu. In the Bounce dialog, QuickTime will be given as the output file format whilst the audio files can be exported either in Stereo Interleaved or Mono Summed format. You can also select the resolution and sample rate for the audio conversion. When you click on the Bounce button, a file selector dialog box will appear. Assign a path to your new QuickTime movie. When you click Save, a new movie capable of being read by all applications that support QuickTime will be written in real time to your hard disk.

AVoption|XL

Whilst the Import QuickTime function is flawless in its operation, it's unsuitable for professional applications because broadcast-quality video material is required in post-production and QuickTime cannot approach that quality. Instead, Digidesign has fallen back on its family ties with Avid Technology and is offering AVoption|XL, an optional soft-/hardware combination.

AVoption|XL is based on the Meridien hardware from Avid and is therefore compatible with the DV systems Symphony, Media Composer|XL and Xpress NT. The hardware consists of the Meridien digital media board, a PCI card, and a breakout box offering connections for component-, composite- and S-video that can also be fitted with SDI inputs. When this is combined with the supplied software, the function range of Pro Tools is expanded to such an extent that in addition to the capture, import and playback of Avid-compatible video and 24P clips, NTSC and PAL-based video material can be loaded directly into the Pro Tools software. The AVoption|XL employs the JPEG file interchange format (JFIF) and supports not only uncompressed image material (1:1) but also other quality levels including 15:1 compression. It is also possible to import multiple video clips into the Pro Tools video track.

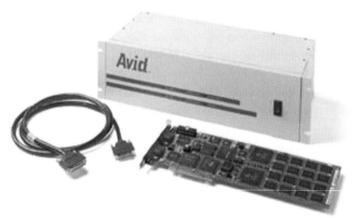

AVoption|XL offers an unprecedented level of integration between audio and video

Recording Video Data

Just as when you're recording audio or MIDI data, you must begin by creating a track to hold the video data. Select New Avid Movie Track (New Movie Track in Pro Tools 6.0 or lower) from the Movie menu, and a video track will appear in the Edit window. Since this video track contains no mixing functions, it is ignored by the Mix window. Select Display › Edit window Shows I/O view.

Next, prepare the video track for recording by using the track controls in the Edit window. Here's a brief breakdown of the functions of the various individual controls:

- **Track Name** – As you would expect, this field allows you to name the video file.

- **Rec** – Record-enables the video track.

- **View Options** – Toggles the display of the video data between frames and blocks.

- **Track Height** – Opens a pop-up menu containing various display options for the video data.

- **Track Options** – Allows you to select the video format for the recording (NTSC, PAL), the video input (composite, component, S-video, SDI) and the

format for the video output (component, S-video).

- **Compression Level** – Allows you to select a compression level from the pop-up menu.

- **Record Drives 1–3** – Allows you to select the target drive volumes for the video capture. The maximum duration of the recording is displayed directly beneath the button.

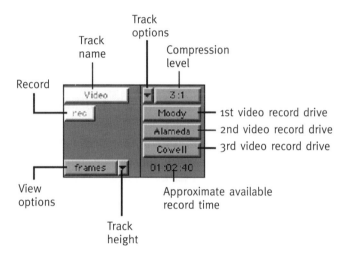

The track controls are used to set up the video track for recording and playback

Movie Recording

Naturally you can create additional audio and/or MIDI tracks in parallel with your recording and record-enable them at the same time. The next step is to position the cursor at the position in the Edit window where you wish to begin recording and activate the Record button in the Transport window. Now commence playback of the video source and click Play in the Pro Tools Transport window. The video data will be recorded to the video track at the same time as the audio is being recorded to the audio and/or MIDI track(s). To terminate the recording process manually, either click the Stop button or press the spacebar on your computer keyboard. If you make several recordings that overlap, the hidden data in the playlist of the

video track will be lost. The data, however, will still be present in the original video file.

Importing Video Data
Avid Import

With AVoption|XL, Pro Tools offers conversion-free media compatibility. It is therefore possible to import broadcast-quality video material from an Avid system into Pro Tools. First, however, the data must be converted to Open Media Framework Interchange (OMFI) format using the DigiTranslator 2.0 software included in the delivery of AVoption|XL. DigiTranslator supports the import and export of OMF media files and sequences and AAF sequences as well as performing the translation of volume data into Pro Tools breakpoint automation playlists. It also translates in the opposite direction, creating sample-accurate exports of Pro Tools audio and session files for Avid and other OMF 2.0- and AAF-capable systems.

AVoption|XL And Video Streaming

Even when AVoption|XL is installed, it remains possible to import QuickTime films. Unlike OMFI videos, which are loaded directly into the video track using the Add Movie command in the Movie menu, QuickTime clips can only be loaded into the session using the Import Movie command. In the course of execution, Pro Tools wipes all existing data from the video track, so QuickTime movies cannot be combined with OMFI videos in Pro Tools.

Multiple Streams

As already mentioned, Pro Tools cannot work with more than one video stream at a time. Certain Avid systems, on the other hand, support simultaneous streams of real-time video. Multi-stream transitions and effects must therefore be rendered in the Avid sequence before being added to Pro Tools, since otherwise Pro Tools will substitute black frames wherever the multi-stream effects occur.

Networking

In the context of a professional post-production setup including both Pro Tools and Avid systems, it is possible to network the workstations using Avid Unity Media Net and Media Manager. Unity is designed as a network solution for storage systems and permits extremely fast data transfer between the different platforms; here, too, the data must be translated into OMFI format.

Editing And Outputting Video Data

Pro Tools offers very limited video editing possibilities. At the end of the day, there would be little point in offering a wide range of functions for the editing of video data within Pro Tools, since Pro Tools workstations are generally manned by sound engineers. Nonetheless Pro Tools operators do need to be able to assign a new time code position to the video data as well as make the occasional cut.

Both these tasks are relatively easy to perform using the editing functions found in the Edit window and menu bar. To spot a video clip to a new frame location, select Time Code from the Display menu. Now enable Spot mode by clicking the Spot button and click the Movie track with the Grabber tool to bring up the Spot dialog. Enter the new SMPTE frame number in the Start field, click on OK and the movie clip will relocate to the desired position.

Deleting

To delete all or part of a clip, select the passage you wish to remove using the Selector tool and then Clear Selection in the Movie menu. The material selected will be removed from the playlist.

Outputting The Project

Obviously when you have finished editing, you will need to output the project. There are two ways of doing this: either you can copy the session to an external master recorder using either the S-video or Component output of the AVoption Breakout Box whilst at the same time outputting the audio mix via your Pro Tools interface, or you can export the entire session using the command Bounce to Disk in the File menu. In the latter case, you should select as your file type OMFI in the Bounce dialog, which is only available if you have AVoption|XL. The result is the creation of an OMFI-compatible file, converted into the correct format for Avid systems by the DigiTranslator..

Synchronisation

Finally we need to discuss another Pro Tools setup for adding sound to video material. In practice it is extremely convenient to be able to load images and sound into a single editor, but it is not strictly necessary, since Pro Tools, like virtually any external multi-track machine, is capable of synchronisation with a video editing system. In such a case, the images are played back exclusively on the video workstation whilst Pro Tools operates in slave mode with frame-accurate synchronicity. What makes this possible is the technology of time code synchronisation upon which we have already touched and which allows the playback speed of one medium to be translated into a timing frequency that all the connected systems can follow. Pro Tools is also capable of interpreting this tempo information although a synchroniser, which is available as an option, is required for the purpose. Digidesign has been producing such devices for some time now but

streamlined the range simultaneously with the introduction of the IHD systems. The SMPTE Slave Driver (SSD) and Video Slave Driver (VSD) – though not the Universal Slave Driver (USD) – have been discontinued and replaced by the SYNC I/O, which can perform all the same tasks as the older models.

The SYNC I/O can process all commonly-used formats and provides for the synchronisation of Pro Tools to external audio and video machines

House Sync

It is also advisable to install a house sync generator to act as a central reference for both the video editor and the Pro Tools hardware. This ensures that the hardware timing signals (word clock and video reference) for all the devices communicating with each other are identical.

Master And Slave

Which of the workstations in the system operates as the master and which as the slave depends in any given case upon the task to be performed. If you are adding sound to a finished video film, it makes sense to run the video source as the master, since the film speed serves as the reference for the subsequent use of the material. That means, the video editor should prescribe the time code that will determine the playback speed in Pro Tools via the synchroniser. For this arrangement, it is necessary to configure Pro Tools' transport controls: in the Transport window, in place of Pro Tools select as the new transport master the device in question. The new transport master must first have been defined and enabled in the Synchronisation register of the Peripherals dialog accessed via the Setups menu. Even then, Pro Tools

will not submit to outside control until you switch to online mode, either by selecting Online from the Operations menu or by clicking the Online button in the Transport window. When Pro Tools is online, the incoming time code is evaluated and used to control the transport functions; when Pro Tools is offline, the incoming time code is ignored.

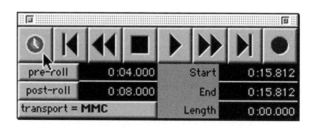

When you switch to Online mode, Pro Tools processes the incoming time code data

Problems In Slave Mode

So far, so good. The operation in slave mode requires the transport functions such as Play, Fast Forward and Rewind to be controlled by the master, but from the point of view of workflow, it is extremely inconvenient to have to control the machine you are working at from the controls of another device, which is why in MachineControl Digidesign has created a software option that allows you to use the serial nine-pin interface of the host computer to output control messages. This allows you to control all transport functions including special ones like Jog and Shuttle via the Pro Tools transport controls and transmit the messages to external machines. In our setup the consequences are as follows:

the transport buttons of the slave device (Pro Tools) control the master device (the video machine), even though it is still the master device that is emitting the time code and the slave (Pro Tools) that is following. In practice, this means that it makes scarcely any difference at all to your manner of working whether Pro Tools is the master or the slave. The only difference in the latter case is that the video workstation is controlling the playback speed as well as the synchronism of Pro Tools.

9 PRO TOOLS AND LOGIC AUDIO

Created by the Hamburg-based software house Emagic, Logic is a widely used MIDI sequencer of which there are several versions – Logic Platinum, Logic Gold... – on the market. Like all programs of its type, Logic has been offering integrated audio functions, that is to say hard disk recording, since the beginning of the '90s. Unlike Pro Tools, which started off as a pure audio program and to which MIDI functions were later added, with Logic it was the other way about, and since Emagic has always aimed to cater for the professional community, a way was quickly found to make use of Pro Tools TDM systems behind the Logic user interface. In other words, Logic is a competitor for Digidesign software but not for its hardware. In the area of professional music production, Logic/TDM systems are now more or less the standard. Naturally it is also possible to use Pro Tools LE hardware (Mbox, Digi 001, Digi 002 and Audiomedia III) with Logic. Since Emagic was taken over by Apple in the Summer of 2002, the development of Logic for Windows has been discontinued.

A Little History

Whereas in the '80s it was necessary to edit MIDI data in software MIDI sequencers such as Steinberg 24 and Notator from C-Lab and synchronise the audio tracks on the tape recorder to it, technological developments at the start of the '90s offered new possibilities: multi-track hard disk recording became affordable and it was decided that it would be more convenient for users if audio tracks were integrated into MIDI sequencers. Only with the integration of TDM systems into Logic did the next horizon come into view: the possibility of regarding audio tracks as something more than building

blocks to be moved around and the integration and mixing of effects from within the software itself. Seen from this historical perspective, it becomes clear why Pro Tools software and Logic are informed by quite different operating concepts.

The Structure Of Logic

Without wanting to go too much into details, the conceptual difference between Pro Tools and Logic essentially reflects the different origins of the two programs. With its roots sunk deep in MIDI, Emagic opted for a MIDI-based operating environment in which all objects that play a part in the program are defined. These environment objects could be anything from MIDI-controlled hardware instruments such as synthesisers to mixer channels for audio tracks. One of the most striking differences between the two applications is that with Logic, unlike with Pro Tools, the tempo is invariably based on beats. Furthermore, in Logic there is not the strict division of functions between different windows that there is between the Edit and Mix windows in Pro Tools. Instead there is an Arrange window, which in many respects resembles the Edit window in Pro Tools, a large number of different editors that can be used to look in some detail at the MIDI and audio material, and the Track Mixer or Environment Layer. It can be difficult for beginners to grasp the fact that they can access the mixer not only from the Track Mixer but also from the Environment.

Logic is modular in structure and capable in many respects of adapting to the needs of the user. Although this may constitute an advantage in the eyes of advanced users, it can be intimidating for beginners. A good example of this is provided by the fact that in Logic the keyboard shortcuts are freely definable, unlike in Pro Tools where they are predefined. It is possible also for users to store their favourite window configurations for particular tasks in the form of *screen sets*.

Driver Concepts
DAE And Direct I/O

The form the integration takes depends upon the Pro Tools hardware used, the options being DAE with TDM or Direct I/O. Logic Audio Platinum even supports multiple audio systems running in parallel. Whilst a Logic TDM system remains the ultimate in MIDI-based music production, Digidesign's Direct I/O is the driver concept for host-based Logic systems.

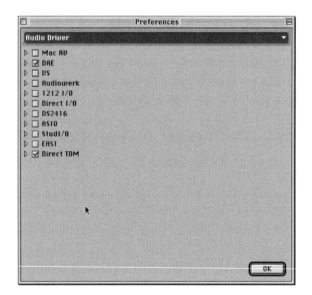

Audio drivers are registered In the Audio Hardware And Drivers window

Integration Via The DAE

TDM systems are integrated via the DAE so that the TDM buss is available within Logic. You can therefore use TDM plug-ins and live inputs and make use of the extensive routing possibilities of the TDM system whilst retaining the user interface of Logic Audio Platinum. In practice there is one conceptual difference that distinguishes working with Pro Tools from working with Logic and it relates to the classification of tracks: where

Pro Tools has aux inputs, audio tracks and master faders, Logic has tracks, inputs, aux sends, busses, outputs and a master fader.

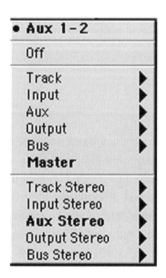

In Logic, audio objects are classified differently

Whilst Logic's tracks are equivalent to Pro Tools' audio tracks, Logic's aux sends and inputs are equivalent to Pro Tools' aux inputs. Logic's outputs and busses are replaced in Pro Tools by master faders. The master fader in Logic, on the other hand, is a higher-ranked object that controls the total volume of audio hardware for all outputs. For all that their systems of classification may differ, in practice it is hard to say that either system yields any particular advantage over that employed by the other.

Platinum Only

The DAE with TDM driver is only available if you are using Logic Audio Platinum as opposed to Gold or Logic Audio. For Pro Tools HD systems, you will need to budget for an additional PT|HD extension, whereas older TDM systems will run under Logic Audio Platinum without needing such add-ons.

Without TDM Via Direct I/O

If your Digidesign hardware does not support TDM or you wish to work within logic without TDM, you can use Logic with a Direct I/O driver. In this case, Logic offers many ways of adapting the system to your requirements. An important parameter in this context is the I/O buffer size, as it has a crucial bearing upon latency values.

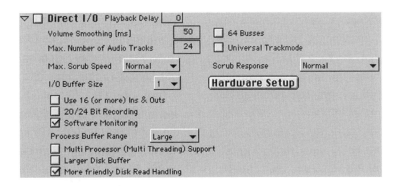

In addition to TDM, there is also a Logic driver for host-based systems: Direct I/O

ESB – The Emagic System Bridge

An important development for Logic TDM systems is the Emagic System Bridge (ESB). This is an extension for Logic Audio Platinum that expands a TDM system by allowing native audio tracks, Logic and VST plug-ins and audio instruments to be routed into Logic's TDM mixer. ESB is not, however, part of Logic Audio Platinum and has to be acquired separately.

ESB Integration

The best way to think of the Emagic System Bridge is as a bridge between the host-based mixer and the TDM mixer that allows users of Pro Tools hardware to combine both native and TDM processing. Unlike the ADAT Bridge, however, the ESB realizes the connection of the two audio systems at the software level. If a Logic TDM system is equipped with ESB, the Direct TDM (DTDM) audio engine is available to it. All audio objects that wish to address this engine need to be routed via the eight outputs in the TDM mixer. In the TDM mixer, an aux send should be used as the input for the ESB channels.

This allows Logic TDM systems, too, to profit from the constantly increasing power of computer CPUs. In addition to VST plug-ins and the excellent effects that Emagic delivers with Logic Audio, this combination offers above all the possibility of integrating numerous software

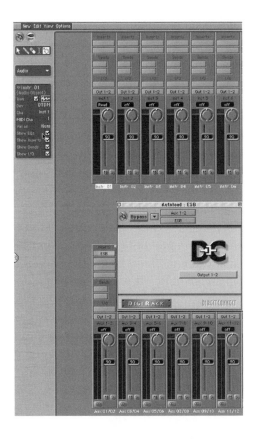

In our example, instruments 1 and following are routed to Outs 1–2 of the DTDM audio engine and Aux 01/02 of our TDM mixer with the ESB plug-in serving as the input

instruments into the TDM mixer. On the one hand, there are the very good software tone generators produced by Emagic itself, such as the EXS 24 sampler, the EVP 88 electric piano and the ES-1 and ES-2 synthesisers. On the other, an ESB system naturally also offers you the option of using VST instruments. The EXS-24-TDM does not have to be routed over the eight ESB channels but can be integrated directing into the aux channels of the TDM mixer. This option is available automatically if you possess the EXS 24 and ESB.

Automation

From the introduction of Pro Tools 4 to that of Logic 5, Digidesign had a clear lead in the domain of automation, but since then, much has happened. Emagic has created a new track-based automation for Logic 5 that also applies the principle of the playlist to automation. Now it is even possible in Logic to display several automation playlists for a track simultaneously. In terms of automation resolution, Logic has also made clear advances: previously this was limited to 128 steps (the MIDI norm) but now, in theory, up to 32 bits are possible. In practice, it appears that Pro Tools still enjoys a slight lead since the improved resolution in Logic so far only applies to the volume parameter of a channel strip, whereas in Pro Tools higher resolution is also available for plug-in parameters.

10 COMPATIBILITY AND PERIPHERALS

In addition to the principal themes with which we have dealt in the preceding chapters, there are a few miscellaneous subjects connected with Pro Tools that need to be addressed, such as the way Pro Tools interacts with the outside world – whether we are talking about the compatibility of the various Pro Tools systems with each other, the networking of several systems over the internet or the compatibility of Pro Tools with other video and audio systems – and the range of control surfaces and other peripherals that have been produced to make life easier for Pro Tools operators.

Compatibility Between Pro Tools Systems

Since the name Pro Tools has been with us for many years, there are all manner of different systems floating about that call themselves Pro Tools. There are in fact only three versions of the software: Pro Tools Free, Pro Tools LE and Pro Tools, but since the three types of software and also the hardware components that are available have different characteristics, complete compatibility was never going to be an easy thing to achieve. Then there is the fact that Pro Tools is available on both platforms, the Mac and the PC. When we speak of compatibility in this context, what we are referring to is the feasibility of editing on System A sessions created on System B when the two systems are equipped differently.

Let it be said at the outset: Pro Tools is exemplary in this respect. Digidesign is way ahead of most other audio programs for PC and Mac that admit of different hardware configurations. Nonetheless there are one or two situations that can lead to problems for the inexperienced user.

Exchanging Between Mac And PC

When creating a new session, you can guarantee the integrity of data exchange between Mac and PC at no cost simply by selecting the option Enforce Mac/PC Compatibility. This will ensure that all audio files are stored in WAV format and not as Sound Designer II documents, as was once commonly the case on the Mac.

Systems Of Different Sizes

In addition to the question of compatibility between the Mac and PC platforms, there is the issue of session exchange between differently specified Pro Tools systems. If, for example, you have created a session with 64 audio tracks using a Pro Tools Mix system, you will not be able to play back the session in full using either Pro Tools Free or Pro Tools LE, since the playback capacity of Pro Tools LE systems is 32 tracks and that of Pro Tools Free, eight. Despite this, Pro Tools can still open sessions without any difficulty, even though they may exceed the resources of the current system. All that happens is that Pro Tools deactivates the tracks that cannot be played back on the current system. In our hypothetical case, Pro Tools LE will simply play back 32 of the 64 tracks and deactivate the other 32, whereas Pro Tools Free will play back only eight.

Which Eight?

By default, Pro Tools selects the tracks in numerical order (1, 2, etc) until it reaches system capacity and then deactivates the remainder, but you can override the default manually and decide for yourself which tracks are to be played back – always subject to system capacity. When you finish editing, save the session and transfer it back to a larger system, the original resources will still be available. The same principle holds for other system components such as plug-ins, inputs and outputs: whatever is not available on the current system is deactivated and only reactivated when the resources again become available, that is when you switch back to a larger system. In other worlds, you can edit on a smaller system a session created on a larger one without truncating it; the smaller systems are therefore fully compatible with the larger ones, and that, as we have already remarked, is exemplary.

Plug-ins

With plug-ins as well – provided both interfaces are available, which is only the case with TDM systems – you can switch between the RTAS and TDM plug-in interface, and even in this scenario, we have never encountered any compatibility problems in practice.

DigiStudio

With the advent of the World Wide Web, the possibility of exchanging musical data over the Rocket Network and, in effect, working 'live' together over the Internet became a real one. It took a while for Digidesign to implement Rocket functionality into the Pro Tools software. The way it worked was that you opened an account at www.digipronet.com that entitled you to store a certain quantity of data on an Internet server and to a certain amount of data throughput. Digidesign offered a range of deals, the cheapest costing around £6 ($10) per month and entitling users to 300MB of throughput per month along with up to 50MB of storage capacity. That was admittedly not all that much, but the Vorbis algorithm that came with DigiStudio could be used, rather like MP3, to compress the data. The initiator could invite as many people as he or she liked to collaborate on the project. Several people could even work together on the same session. To avoid data chaos, however, only one person was able to edit a given track at a given time; in such cases he was said to have the 'ownership' of the track.

Which person was awarded the ownership of which tracks, including the right to create as well as edit them, was determined by the initiator of the session, who was not obliged to make every last track available for editing nor even for playback.

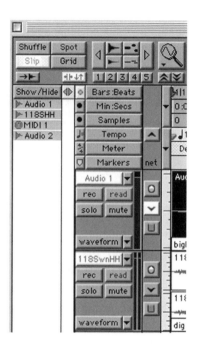

When using DigiStudio, the Net View column is added to Pro Tools' Edit window

Program Integration

The integration of DigiStudio functionality into the Pro Tools interface was well realized. Beneath the toolbar in the Edit window were the global Upload and Download arrows used to transmit all changes to the online session to and from the server. A further characteristic of the Pro Tools software versions that supported DigiStudio were the so-called Net View controls, which could be displayed in both the Edit and Mix windows of Pro Tools and contained extensive information about the status of the track. You could decide individually for each track, whether and what degree of compression should be applied before the upload or download to the online session. All the commands and options relating to the DigiStudio functionality were conveniently located in the File › Collaborate Via DigiStudio sub menu.

Exchanging Other Data

With DigiStudio, it was not simply the raw audio data that was exchanged but all the elements of the session. These included the plug-ins and their settings, MIDI tracks and naturally automation data as well. DigiStudio

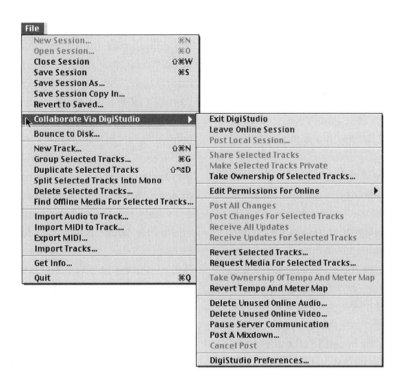

All the DigiStudio functions are shown at a glance in the Collaborate Via DigiStudio drop-down menu

was therefore superior to many of the other solutions intended to overcome the geographical separation between producers and musicians or between ADR directors and speakers. The takes were directly integrated into the session and could be processed with the desired effects. You could virtually work live or else make time differences work to your advantage: whilst the producer in Europe was sleeping, a musician in California could be laying down tracks. At breakfast, the producer could check the results and send the musician messages and perhaps suggest improvements, which he in turn would download over breakfast and act upon. In other words, the project could be advancing on a 24-hour a day basis without anyone losing any sleep.

Rocket Network Shuts Down...

Sadly, on 31 March 2003, the Rocket Network, upon whose infrastructure the DigiStudio and DigiDelivery services were dependent, was forced to shut down its servers, blaming the difficult economic climate and the

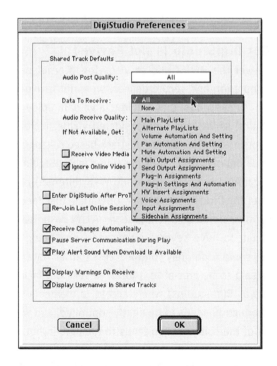

Not only raw audio files but plug-ins and their settings as well as automation data could be exchanged using DigiStudio

slow adoption of the paid service. Users were credited with the existing balance of their accounts. 'We still believe deeply in the dream of music and post-production communities working on a project simultaneously from anywhere in the world,' commented President and CEO, Pam Miller, and Willy Henshall, Founder and Chairman, in a joint statement.

...And Is Acquired By Avid...

On 4 April 2003, Avid Technology, Inc, announced that it had acquired the assets of the Rocket Network. 'Rocket Network developed technology that has greatly excited and creatively charged the Digidesign Pro Tools audio community,' commented Dave Lebolt, vice president and general manager of Digidesign. 'By integrating this technology into our current offerings, we plan to provide Pro Tools customers, who are the world's leading producers of audio media, the means to take advantage of smooth, collaborative workflow between Pro Tools systems over local area networks or the Internet. With powerful tools for easy and secure digital delivery of large media files of any type, including audio or video, this new technology will help our customers move vast amounts of media over the Web at high speed.'

...But DigiStudio Is Not Revived

However the DigiStudio services for internet based collaboration and secure delivery were not revived, as the business model that required large data uploads to a central server was not considered viable. Instead it was planned to incorporate the track-based collaboration and digital delivery capabilities found in DigiStudio into a Local Area Network (LAN)- and WAN (Internet)-based model for Pro Tools systems, obviating the need for data to be stored on a central server. A LAN-based system was felt to have several advantages, one being that users could absolutely control access to their data. This was said to be crucial to a lot of larger post facilities (such as film studios) where access to elements used in production needs to be tightly controlled, and where a lot of the collaboration tends to happen 'in house'.

Pro Tools Hardware Controllers

Pro Tools offers the entire functionality of a professional studio in the form of software – and

that, precisely, is the problem. Many operators do not enjoy using the mouse and professional users, in particular, are used to operating with larger user interfaces. The range of what are called 'mix controllers' for Pro tools, such as remote controls with integrated faders, is very large and runs from conventional MIDI controllers to the dedicated control surfaces Control 24 and Pro Control offered by Digidesign itself. In addition to differences in terms of ease-of-use, there are considerable differences in price between the various options. Among the most affordable MIDI controllers, for example, is the JL Cooper CS-10, which however has no motorised faders. Priced at around £600 ($1,000), The Motor Mix from CM Labs is another of the more economical options. It does offer motorised faders but they are not touch-sensitive.

Emagic Logic Control And Mackie Control

Emagic's Logic Control, which costs around £900 ($1,500), offers another way of controlling Pro tools (using a Mackie HUI emulation). If you mainly work within Logic and only occasionally with the Pro Tools software, you will be grateful for the HUI emulation, as it enhances Logic Control. The very similar Mackie Control also offers Pro Tools integration at an attractive price.

Mackie HUI

The original HUI from Mackie communicates better in this respect with Pro Tools but at around £4,000 ($7,000)is considerably more expensive although it does offer additional features (two mic preamps, talkback, monitoring, a special level meter display).

Control 24 And Pro Control

Digidesign itself offers the most expensive controllers for Pro Tools in the shape of the Control 24 and Pro Control. In contrast to the other solutions, these communicate with the computer not via MIDI but via Ethernet. Since a Control 24 costs around £7,500 ($12,800) and a Pro Control £11,500 ($19,300), great things inevitably are expected, but whilst the Control 24 is equipped with 16 microphone preamps, integrated talkback and monitoring functions that turn Pro Tools

Digidesign's thoroughbred mix controllers Pro Control (left) and Control 24 (below) are not cheap

into more or less the perfect studio, Pro Control, despite its modularity and some very good extras, does not represent especially good value for money. Both controllers run the Pro Tools software at a resolution of 1,024 steps per fader, which makes for highly precise programming and automation.

Whilst Pro Tools is only available for TDM systems and Digidesign's Digi 002 with its integrated mix controller was custom designed for the purpose, the Control 24 can also be used with LE systems.

Machine Control And Digi Translator

Even though they are not standard components of any Pro Tools system, Machine Control and Digi Translator are likely soon enough to appear on your shopping list if you are working in post-production.

Machine Control is a software extension of Pro Tools systems that facilitates the communication with external equipment. With the help of Machine Control, you can, for example, operate the transport functions (start, stop, rewind, fast forward) of video recorders from your Pro Tools workstation using simple keyboard commands. If you are using Pro Tools 5.1 or higher, it is also possible to operate Pro Tools in slave mode receiving Sony nine-pin commands from an external machine operating as transport master. The only drawback is the price of £520 ($870). If, however, you are working in a post-production studio with external video recorders or other tape machines, this option is indispensable.

Digi Translator, meanwhile, is primarily designed to optimise data exchange with Avid video systems (audio and/or video). Here the Open Media Framework Interchange (OMFI) plays a key role. The system also makes it possible to transfer sessions to and from Logic Audio Platinum. To export a session for use by another program, it must first be stored as an OMF file and you can decide whether or not to save the audio files as part of the session. This option is useful if you are intending to transfer the session to another workstation. If all you are intending to do is switch to a different application at the same workstation, you should limit the transfer to the reference information to prevent the file becoming unnecessarily large.

OMFI Data

OMFI bears a certain resemblance to General MIDI, since OMFI not only ensues that the audio files of other programs are recognised but also that the playlists are correctly displayed in the tracks. Both OMFI and General MIDI represent an attempt to define a common standard based on the highest common multiple. With Avid programs (for example, the widely used Media Composer) even automation data is transferred via Digi Translator. Digi Translator has replaced the so-called OMF tool and costs around £300 ($500).

PRE, SYNC I/O And MIDI I/O

When Digidesign introduced the new HD hardware, three additional peripheral devices were presented that were designed to supply the missing links in the production chain. Whilst SYNC I/O replaced the Universal Slave Driver (USD) and is needed for synchronisation with external equipment, PRE and MIDI I/O are products for which there was no precedent in the Digidesign product range.

PRE is an eight-channel microphone preamp system that combines outstanding sound quality with ease-of-use. Besides microphone signals, it allows you to process line and instrument level signals. The great thing about PRE, however, is the fact that it can be controlled remotely either by the Pro Tools software or by Pro Control or Control 24. This allows you to place the microphone preamp in the recording room so that the weak microphone signal does not have to travel far. The remote control of PRE from within Pro Tools also provides a way of storing its settings.

MIDI I/O is a rather less spectacular device but nonetheless one that is worthy of mention, namely a multi-port MIDI interface. It is connected to the computer via the USB and with its ten MIDI inputs and outputs allows a considerable number of hardware tone generators and/or PRE modules to be integrated into your Pro Tools environment and remote-controlled via MIDI.

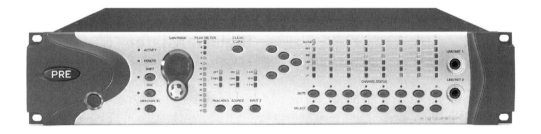

Digidesign's PRE offers eight remote-controlled microphone preamps

11 SELF-HELP

In this chapter, we would like to offer a little help to get you started as well as some tips in case your system does not function quite as smoothly as it ought to. We will explain the basic procedures for installing the hardware and software as well as providing you with some basic information on the subject of hard disks. We will also look at the most common error reports and troubleshooting techniques for when things go wrong.

Hardware Installation
Choice Of Computer

With the exception of Mbox and Digi 002, which connect to the computer via the USB and FireWire ports respectively, the installation of Pro Tools inevitably involves opening up your computer to install at least one PCI card. Before you begin, however, you should make sure that the computer you are planning to use has been approved by Digidesign for the use of Pro Tools. An overview of the system requirements is provided at the beginning of the next chapter, but for a more detailed description you should consult the Digidesign website www.digidesign.com where you will find a list of the computers Digidesign recommends sorted by Pro Tools systems and platform (Mac or PC).

Naturally, it is possible that Pro Tools systems will work with computers other than those included on the Digidesign list, but the risk in such cases is yours and such experiments are generally unadvisable. Unfortunately there are very few Digidesign-approved computers for Windows.

Inserting The PCI Card

Once you have the right computer, you need to insert the PCI card(s). Before unpacking the card, make sure

to discharge any static electricity in your body by touching a radiator or something similar with your bare hand. This is to avoid damaging the card. The next thing to do is to remove the metal cover of the PCI slot at the back of the computer so that you will be able to connect the PCI card(s) to the audio interfaces and other peripherals. Now, holding the PCI card by the top edge, carefully insert it into the requisite slot, though which this is varies depending upon the computer model and the PCI card itself. Pay careful attention to the Digidesign instructions especially when installing TDM systems.

Connecting The Audio Interface

The next step is to connect the audio interface(s) to the PCI card using the cable supplied. When planning the installation, pay attention to the length of the cable. The cables supplied for connecting the audio interfaces are not especially long, but cables up to 30m in length for HD systems are available from the DigiStore. A cable that length, however, will cost you around £180 extra.

TDM Buss

With TDM systems, after installing the individual PCI cards, you have to ensure that they are connected to the TDM buss. This is done using another specialised cable. MIX systems and their predecessors were connected using flat ribbon cables, and the cable specified the number of cards that could be connected. You had to use special cables provided by Digidesign. Ordinary flat ribbon cables from a PC store, unfortunately, would not do the trick.

For the TDM II architecture of the HD systems, Digidesign came up with a somewhat more flexible principle for connecting to the TDM. All the cards now possess two TDM connectors and are delivered with a TDM connection cable, so that neighbouring cards are connected with a single cable.

Test Installation

Once all the cards have been inserted and all the necessary connections established, use the DigiTest software provided to see whether the PCI cards have been correctly installed and in the right order.

Audio Interface Calibration

To facilitate the adaptation of the audio interfaces to your studio environment, Digidesign supplies various example sessions. This process, which is called 'calibration', serves primarily to ensure that the level displays of the individual studio components are correctly attuned to each other. The process of calibration is different for each audio interface. Many of the available audio interfaces do not lend themselves to calibration, but are programmed to fixed values.

Software Installation

The installation of the software for a Pro Tools system is generally straightforward. You insert the supplied CD ROM into your CD ROM drive, double click the installation program and all the essential components of the Pro Tools system will be installed automatically. But wait! Before inserting the supplied CD ROM into your drive, make sure that your computer's operating system is ready for the installation of the Pro Tools software. Newly installed operating systems with the default settings usually work best. Bear in mind that other system components such as additional graphics cards, game controllers and so on could lead to compatibility problems with Pro Tools. When you have completed the installation of all the necessary components, you need to complete the authorisation process. The first time you run the software, Pro Tools will prompt you for the serial number provided by Digidesign. Whether or not there are any other queries, depends upon the hardware being used.

When you've performed these basic tasks, you can turn your attention to the installation and authorisation of your plug-ins. If you possess a large arsenal of additional plug-ins, you can expect this process to take half or even an entire day. The installation of the individual plug-ins, however, is fairly uncomplicated. On the Plug-ins CD ROM, you will find an installation program, which, when you double click on it, will install the plug-in in the Plug-ins sub-folder of the DAE folder as well as installing the supplied presets in the Plug-in Settings sub-folder.

Copy Protection

A great inconvenience from the user's point of view is the fact that all plug-ins (TDM, RTAS and AudioSuite) are copy-protected. This copy protection is generally assured by one of three procedures:

Floppy Disk

The authorisation of plug-ins via floppy disk is now very old-fashioned. When this procedure is used, one of your hard disks will be authorised for the use of the plug-in. This authorisation can be copied back to the floppy disk, for example, if you wish to install the plug-in on a different disk, but this system has various disadvantages. The first is that floppy disks are mechanically vulnerable and tend to break down when you most need them. Once, when changing systems, we had to send back no fewer than ten defective floppy disks to the manufacturers, even though these disks had only been used once (for the installation). Since the hard disk is, so to speak, 'mechanically' authorised, you have to live with the risk of losing that authorisation if ever the disk crashes. Depending upon the licence conditions imposed by the manufacturer in question, you may even be charged for your replacement authorisation.

Challenge/Response

With this modern procedure, an individual challenge code that takes the form of an apparently random series of letters is generated for the hard disk based on various system parameters. The user sends this code to the address given by the plug-in manufacturer (it is obviously quickest to do this via e-mail) and then receives a similarly random-looking series of letters in response.

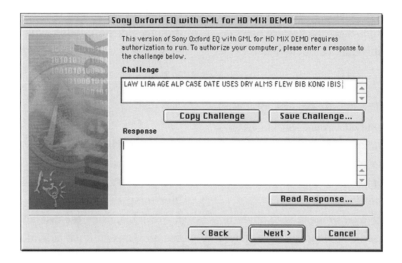

The challenge code is generated automatically and the manufacturer sends you the response. You just have to enter it correctly

The advantage of this procedure lies in the reduced risk of losing the authorisation or succumbing to mechanical problems. If, for example, you inadvertently format the hard disk containing your plug-in authorisation, the plug-in will generate the same challenge code when you reload it and you must then enter the response code supplied by the manufacturer again. The only snags are that you do have to enter the often long codes correctly, and you can only assign your plug-ins to a single hard disk. The licence holder of the plug-in cannot carry his authorisation about with him.

iLok

The latest method of copy protection is based on a small USB hardware key called an iLok, capable of accommodating up to 100 plug-in authorisations and affording mobility to the user of the plug-ins. The authorisations can find their way onto smart key by various routes, the most common being licence cards supplied with the plug-ins that contain a GSM format license chip that has to be detached and which you then insert into the iLok key when prompted by the software. Another approach that is technically feasible would be to authorise the iLok plug via challenge/response or serial number. The danger with smart keys, of course, is that you might lose them.

When you purchase a Pro Tools HD system, the iLok plug comes with it; in all other cases, you have to purchase it separately. The going rate for an iLok seems to be around £40.

Hard Disks

Among the most important components in a hard-disk recording system like Pro Tools are the hard disks themselves. It is they that are primarily responsible for determining how many tracks you can play back at a time. The current upper limit of 32 simultaneous audio tracks on LE systems poses no problems for most modern hard disks. There is, however, an important limitation: it is not just the number of tracks being played back at any one time that is important but the edit density of those tracks that affects the performance of the hard disk. To give you an example, if you are playing back a session in which every track consists of a single region, the read/write head of the hard disk will have considerably less work to do that it would if the tracks contained numerous cuts and fades. If you are using a single hard disk, at a certain critical level, the edit density of the session can render the simultaneous playback of 32 tracks problematic. Whether or not the hard-disk is able to cope depends primarily upon its speed and state of maintenance as well as the buss system used. However Pro Tools supports the use of multiple hard disks, which naturally eases the burden on individual components.

SCSI Or IDE?

SCSI and IDE are two different buss systems for linking your hard disk to your computer. Within each of system, however, there are numerous different protocols that affect the speed of data transfer. FireWire hard disks are also IDE models that employ a special converter to communicate with the FireWire interface.

Digidesign continues to recommend SCSI drives for optimal performance based on the fact that SCSI drives offer advantages over IDE disks at high edit densities. To achieve the highest possible track count, you therefore need to acquire a special SCSI card approved by Digidesign. When you add the cost of this to the cost of the SCSI drives themselves, which are considerably more expensive than IDE drives, you can arrive at a considerable sum. In our experience, however, you can get by perfectly well with the far less expensive FireWire, and internal IDE, hard disks. Our tip is therefore to spare yourself the expense of investing in expensive SCSI hardware and test the performance of your system with an IDE hard disk and either combine it with the fastest buss you can lay your hands on (66MHz minimum) or mount it in a FireWire case. The hard disk itself should be state-of-the-art and rotate at least 7200 RPM. For extremely demanding applications, you can even use two or three IDE drives, provided your computer supports them.

Defragmentation

Hard disks are especially prone to poor performance when they are not properly maintained. One of the most important maintenance tasks is defragmentation, since with the course of time, blocks of data become fragmented and the pieces scattered all over the hard disk with islands of empty space between them. This tends to happen when you delete files individually. The more empty space there is on the hard disk, the harder it is for the read/write head of the hard disk to locate the data, and this impairs performance. The effect of defragmentation is to assemble the scattered pieces of data and write them to one continuous block,

so that the read head does not need to keep jumping around. Norton Utilities, which are available for both PC and Mac, include a very effective defragmenter. Of course, if the capacity of your hard disk is considerable, 60 GB or more, you will have to be patient as defragmentation takes time.

Multiple Hard Disks

With TDM systems, capable of recording and playing back considerably more than 32 tracks it is a good idea to spread the data load over several hard disks. In Pro Tools, using the disk allocation dialog field, you can assign each track individually to a particular hard disk for recording. Unfortunately it is not possible to distribute audio files belonging to a single session to hard disks of different types; you can use either SCSI hard disks or FireWire hard disks but not both at the same time. The Round Robin Allocation function facilitates the task of ensuring that your data streams are shared out equitably between the available drives.

You should try to avoid recording audio on the hard disk that contains the operating system of your computer; the performance is invariably inferior to that obtained elsewhere. If all your other disks are full, however, or you only have one disk, it is possible to use the system disk.

Errors

Here we have tried to list the problems that the technical support personnel encounter most frequently.

Problem – *DAE Error #6042 message during playback within Pro Tools*

Solution – DAE error #6042 indicates that the PCI buss is overloaded. Relief can take various forms: SCSI cards should be switched to 10MHz or less and the ultra mode deactivated. Set the monitor to 256 colours or less and switch off QuickPunch, since this function imposes twice the burden on the PCI buss of a normal voice. Automation data, in particular that of TDM plug-ins, also claims bandwidth on the PCI buss. It may help therefore to thin the automation or partially remove it. Apple blue-and-white G3 computers should be run with Mac OS 8.6 and ROM Version 1.1 or better.

If you are using an ATI graphics card, switch the ATI graphics accelerator off. Often these problems appear when an expansion chassis is being used with TDM systems. In such cases, there are many other possible causes such as PCI cards installed in the wrong order and hardware incompatibility to name but two.

Problem – With Logic Audio 4.6 and Digi 001 on a Windows system, you get the error reports Error #6002, 'Can't initialise Direct I/O', or #6010, 'Could not create DAE deck'

Solution – When you see error message #6002, go into My Computer › Control Panel › Multimedia › Devices Tab › Open Audio Devices › and double-click on Audio for Digidesign Multimedia devices. Choose Do not use audio features on this device and Do not map through this device. Click on Apply and OK to exit. The problem occurs because Logic Audio is using Direct I/O and not the Windows operating system's preferred multimedia record/playback. When enabled and set to Digidesign, Logic Audio can't access the hardware.

Error report #6010 appears when you attempt to launch Logic Audio without having installed WaveDriver and/or Pro Tools software. In this case, Logic cannot initialise Direct I/O because there is no hardware to access.

Problem – How can I optimise my hard disk for the use of Pro Tools under Windows?

Solution – Be sure to use FAT 32 and not FAT/FAT 16, which only permit partitions of two GB. FAT 32 partitions can be far larger and make it easier to maintain a clear overview of the large quantities of data found on the large hard-disks used nowadays. Use larger sectors for your audio partitions (16 or 32K). Most formatting programs use 4K sectors as standard for large partitions. Whilst this setting is very good for large hard disks containing a multitude of small files, it impairs the performance of the hard disk when Pro tools is running. Smaller sectors require the hard disk to be accessed more frequently to read the same quantity of data. Most formatting tools offer you the option of varying the sector size. If possible select 32K.

'Error #9073 Disk too slow' reports can be avoided if you increase the DAE buffer size in the Setups menu. The setting '4' will help in most cases but you have a particularly large number of edits, it may be necessary to select '8' – especially if the disk is not especially fast to start off with. Larger buffer sizes offer the hard disk earlier access to the data. Unfortunately they also increase the reaction time to the Start and Stop commands. Sharing the data load between several hard disks is another way of eliminating such reports.

If you are using hard disk partitions of four GB or more, it is a good idea to limit the recording time for the individual tracks to reduce the reaction time to the Start and Stop commands. By limiting the recording time – by means of a timeline selection, for example – you stipulate that recording should cease as soon as the right hand edge of the selection is reached.

Problem – The application terminates unexpectedly with the Error #2 (Apple computers only)

Solution – This is a Mac OS error that is best remedied by reinstalling both the operating system and the application.

Problem – The function Consolidate Selection is greyed out and cannot therefore be used, even though you have made a timeline selection

Solution – This function is only available if you have the AudioSuite Invert/Duplicate plug-in in your Plug-ins folder, since the consolidation of regions is based on the duplication of regions.

First Aid

One of the reasons Pro Tools systems are so popular is that they are very stable. Nonetheless it can happen that the interaction of the numerous hardware and software components cause the system to malfunction or to function imperfectly. Digidesign undertakes to provide you, as a purchaser, with technical support provided you register your system with the company. For this reason, when you purchase a Pro Tools system you should immediately fill in the registration card included with the purchase and send it in. If you should experience difficulties, please refer the problem first to your local dealer; only if you can see that he is out of his depth should you contact Digidesign's technical support team in the UK. The basic rule is this: in the case of all LE products, you have the right to free support for 90 days from the date of purchase, and in the case of TDM products, the period is a year. Subsequently, you can still obtain technical support but you are charged by the minute.

Here's a word of advice: The support hotline is frequently busy. You can, however, leave a message on the answering machine and someone from the support team will call you back. Be sure to leave your name and telephone number and to speak clearly. Bear in mind, however, that Digidesign support personnel will in future no longer reply to questions the answer to which is in the documentation supplied with the purchase.

In addition to the above-mentioned sources of assistance, there is the Digidesign web site, which is full of useful advice for solving system problems. On the Support page, you will find, among other things, handbooks in .PDF file format, the Digidesign Answerbase, where a number of contextual problems are discussed, the User Conference, which is a means for users to help each other, Compatibility Documents that list which components are compatible with which, as well as a Downloads section from which you can download updates for various system components.

The Digidesign web site at www.digidesign.com is a veritable encyclopaedia of useful information. As well as DigiStudio, a number of other services are available from www.digipronet.com, which serves the pro audio branch. You can, for example, purchase samples on line, enter your name and contact details in a directory intended to be the 'Yellow Pages of the audio industry' and much more.

Pro Tools Mailing Lists

daw-mac@yahoogroups.com
logic-tdm@yahoogroups.com

12 SYSTEM OVERVIEW

In this chapter we would like to offer some advice relating to the acquisition of Digidesign hardware. Not all computers are suitable for music production, still less up to the special demands that Digidesign hardware and software will impose. In addition, we offer an introduction to the hardware that is available from Digidesign and how the various components fit together. Finally we provide information about the second-hand market, since even relatively old Pro Tools hardware and software can be of enormous assistance to the practising musician.

System Requirements

Pro Tools was originally developed for the Apple Macintosh. With the passage of time, however, Digidesign was forced to acknowledge that although the Mac may be very popular among certain groups of the population – creative artists in particular – sales of the Macintosh were always going to lag a long way behind those of the Wintel camp. For this reason, when Version 5.0 of Pro Tools was launched, Digidesign released a version of the same software for Windows-based systems, so as to be able to serve a wider clientele. Whilst the hardware used on both platforms may be identical, there are considerable differences in the two computer environments. The software has therefore had to be adapted considerably as the Mac and Windows operating systems often approach the same task from quite different angles, and this has meant in turn that the implementation of various features of the system on the Windows platform has either been delayed or abandoned. Digidesign is anxious to eliminate or reduce to a minimum all divergence between Mac and PC versions of its software, but it is not known at this time whether important functions such as QuickTime Import will ever be available on the Windows platform.

Very few Wintel computers conform to a defined specification, so there is far less consistency in the way they are equipped than there is with Mac computers. Where reliability is concerned, Digidesign imposes standards to which only a limited group of high-quality and highly priced Windows computers could ever aspire. With computers you have cobbled together yourself or picked up cheaply in the high street, problems are inevitable.

In the following sections, arranged by Digidesign hardware, we set out the minimum system configurations for both the Macintosh and Windows platforms. Please bear in mind that this type of information can very quickly become out-of-date and that, with computers, the turnover of new models is so rapid that a particular model may sometimes be replaced or withdrawn within weeks of its appearance on the market and thereafter difficult if not impossible to lay your hands on. The best place to look for really up-to-date and detailed information on this subject is the Digidesign web site in the section on compatibility.

Pro Tools|HD – Apple Power Macintosh System Requirements

- HD hardware: HD1 (1 core card), HD2 (1 core card, 1 process card), HD3 (1 core card, 2 process cards)

- At least one Digidesign HD audio interface (192 I/O, 192 Digital I/O, 96 I/O)

- Digidesign software: Pro Tools 5.3.1. for Macintosh (supplied)

- OMS 2.3.8 (supplied)

- Apple QuickTime 5.0.2 (supplied)

- ATTO Express Pro Tools 2.7 (supplied)

- Power Macintosh G4 (AGP graphic card) or Titanium Power Book G4 (with Magma CB4DRQ-D1 4-slot CardBuss PCI expansion system)

- Operating system: Mac OS 9.1, 9.2, 9.2.1 or 9.2.2 (depending upon CPU), OS X

- At least 256MB RAM (with high track counts or a high edit density, proportionately more)

- At least one hard disk (IDE or SCSI) for audio data; disk drive rotational speed: 7200 RPM or faster (SCSI drives also require a SCSI card)

- Colour monitor with a resolution of at least 1,024 x 768 pixels

Pro Tools|HD – Windows XP System Requirements

- HD hardware: systems HD1 (Core Card), HD 2 (1 Core, 1 Process card), HD3 (1 Core, 2 Process cards)

- At least one Digidesign HD audio interface (192 I/O, 192 Digital I/O, 96 I/O)

- Digidesign software: Pro Tools 5.3.1 for Windows (supplied)

- OMS 2.3.8 (supplied)

- Apple QuickTime 5.0.2 (supplied)

- Compaq EVO W8000 or IBM IntelliStation M Pro 6850

- Operating system: Windows XP (Home or Professional Edition)

- At least 256MB RAM (with high track counts, a high

edit density, or for better video playback performance, proportionately more)

- At least one hard disk (IDE or SCSI) for audio data; disk drive rotational speed: 7200 RPM or faster (SCSI drives also require a SCSI card)

- Colour monitor with a resolution of at least 1,024 x 768 pixels

Pro Tools|24 MIX – Power Macintosh System Requirements

- MIX hardware: systems: MIX (Core Card), MIXplus (1 Core, 1 MIX Farm card), MIX3 (1 Core, 2 MIX Farm cards)

- At least one Digidesign audio interface (888|24 I/O, 888 I/O, 882|20 I/O, 882 I/O, 1622 I/O, 24-bit ADAT Bridge I/O, ADAT Bridge I/O)

- Digidesign software: Pro Tools 5.1.3 for Macintosh (supplied), 5.2 for DigiStudio

- OMS 2.3.8 (supplied)

- Apple QuickTime 4.1.2 (supplied) or 5.0.2

- ATTO Express Pro Tools 2.3.2 or higher (supplied)

- Power Macintosh G4 (AGP or PCI graphic card), Power Macintosh blue-and-white G3, Power Macintosh beige G3, Power Macintosh 9500/9600, PowerBook G4 (with Magma 2 or 4 Slot CardBuss PCI Expansion System)

- Operating system: Mac OS v9.04, 9.1, 9.2, 9.2.1 or 9.2.2 (depending upon CPU), OS X

- At least 256MB RAM (with large numbers of tracks, high edit density or use of MachineControl, Digi Translator, AVoption or the like, proportionately more)

- At least one hard disk (IDE or SCSI) for audio data; disk drive rotational speed: 7200 RPM or faster (SCSI drives also require a SCSI card)

- Colour monitor with a resolution of at least 1,024 x 768 pixels

Pro Tools|24 MIX – Windows 2000 System Requirements

- MIX hardware: systems MIX (Core Card), MIXplus (1 Core, 1 MIX Farm card), MIX3 (1 Core, 2 MIX Farm cards)

- At least one Digidesign audio interface (888|24 I/O, 888 I/O, 882|20 I/O, 882 I/O, 1622 I/O, 24-bit ADAT Bridge I/O, ADAT Bridge I/O)

- Digidesign software: Pro Tools 5.3.1 for Windows 2000 (supplied)

- OMS 2.3.8 (supplied)

- Apple QuickTime 4.1.2 (supplied) or 5.0.2

- ATTO ExpressPro Tools 2.3.2 or higher (supplied)

- IBM IntelliStation M Pro 6850; IBM IntelliStation E Pro 6846, IBM IntelliStation M Pro 6889 (both models discontinued)

- Operating system: Windows 2000 Professional (Service Pack 2 or higher)

- At least 256MB RAM (with large numbers of tracks, a high edit density, or for better video playback performance, proportionately more)

- At least one hard disk (IDE or SCSI) for audio data; disk drive rotational speed: 7200 RPM or faster (SCSI drives also require a SCSI card)

- AGP graphic card with 16MB RAM or more

- Colour monitor with a resolution of at least 1,024 x 768 pixels

- SCSI card: ATTO EPCI-DC HBA with firmware v1.66; Adaptec AIC-7899 (Trident II) with BIOS 3.1 (integrated in M Pro 6850); Adaptec AIC-78xx chip set with BIOS 1.3x or higher (integrated in M Pro 6889); Adaptec 2940UW PCI with BIOS 1.3x or higher; Adaptec 3940UW PCI with BIOS 1.3x or higher

Digi 001/Pro Tools LE – Power Macintosh System Requirements

- Digi 001 hardware: PCI card, I/O Box, system cable

- Digidesign software: Pro Tools LE 5.1.1 for Macintosh (supplied)

- OMS 2.3.8 (supplied)

- Apple QuickTime 4.1.2 (supplied) or 5.0.2

- Power Macintosh G4 (AGP or PCI graphic card), Power Macintosh blue-and-white G3, Power Macintosh 9600/200MHz or higher, PowerBook Titanium G4 (with Magma 2 Slot CardBuss PCI Expansion System)

- Operating system: Mac OS v9.04, 9.1, 9.2, 9.2.1 or 9.2.2 (depending upon CPU), OS X

- At least 128; better 192MB RAM (with large numbers of tracks, a high edit density or use of MachineControl, DigiTranslator, AVoption and the like, proportionately more)

- At least one hard disk (IDE or SCSI) for audio data; disk drive rotational speed: 7200 RPM or faster (SCSI drives also require a SCSI card)

- Colour monitor with a resolution of at least 1,024 x 768 pixels

Digi 001/Pro Tools LE – Windows XP Home Edition/Windows 98 SE/Windows Me System Requirements

- Digi 001 hardware: PCI card, I/O Box, system cable

- Digidesign software: Pro Tools LE 5.3.1 for Windows XP (supplied); Pro Tools LE 5.1.1 for Windows 98 SE & Windows Me

- Intel Pentium 4 single processor, 1.3–2GHz; Intel Pentium III single processor with 500MHz or higher; AMD Athlon XP, all single processors; AMD Athlon Thunderbird, all single processors

- Intel processors: Intel chip sets 845, 850 or 860

- Athlon processors: VIA chip sets

- Operating system: Windows XP Home Edition

- At least 256MB RAM (used simultaneously with a MIDI sequencer or, for better video playback performance, proportionately more); better still is 384MB

- ATX motherboard

- At least one hard disk (IDE or SCSI) for audio data; disk drive rotational speed: 7200 RPM or faster (SCSI drives also require a SCSI card)

- AGP graphics card with 16MB RAM or more

- Colour monitor with a resolution of at least 1,024 x 768 pixels

- SCSI card: Adaptec AVA-2906

Please note: Digi 001 is not supported on the following systems or with the following components:

- Motherboards with SiS chip sets (Silicon Integrated Systems)

- Hewlett Packard Pavilion computers

- Computers with the following AMD processors: AMD K6, K6-2/K6-III, K7

- Computers with Intel Pentium I or Pentium II processors

- Motherboards with mixed AMD and VIA chip sets

Mbox/Pro Tools LE – Power Macintosh System Requirements

- Mbox hardware: Mbox, USB cable

- Digidesign software: Pro Tools LE 5.2 for Macintosh (supplied)

- OMS 2.3.8 (supplied)

- Apple QuickTime 5.0.2 (supplied)

- All Power Macintoshes with integrated USB interfaces: all G4 models, G4 Cube, Power Macintosh blue-and-white G3, all iMacs; PowerBook G4, PowerBook G3, iBook

- Operating system: Mac OS 9.1, 9.2, 9.2.1 or 9.2.2 (9.2.2 recommended), OS X

- At least 192; better 256MB RAM

- Colour monitor/laptop screen with a resolution of at least 1,024 x 768 pixels

Pro Tools FREE For Macintosh

- Digidesign software: Pro Tools 5.0.1 FREE for Mac

- OMS 2.3.8 (supplied)

- Apple QuickTime 4.1.2 (supplied) or 5.0.2

- All Power Macintosh G4 models, Power Macintosh blue-and-white G3, all iMacs; PowerBook G3; models from 200MHz: Power Mac Beige G3, 9500, 9600

- Operating system: Mac OS v8.6 to 9.X (depending upon CPU)

- At least 128; better 192MB RAM

- At least one approved hard disk (IDE or SCSI) for audio data (SCSI drives also require a SCSI card)

- Colour monitor with a resolution of at least 1,024 x 768 pixels

Pro Tools FREE For Windows 98/Me

- Digidesign software: Pro Tools 5.0.1 FREE Revision 2 for Windows

- All Intel Pentium III machines with Single processor; Intel Pentium II machines with single processors from 300MHz; Intel Celeron from 300MHz; AMD Athlon Thunderbird processor; AMD Athlon XP processor

- Operating system: Windows Me or 98 Second Edition (Windows XP, 2000, NT, 95, 3.1 is not supported)

- At least 128; better 192MB RAM

- Intel chip set

- Phoenix or Award BIOS (recommended)

- AGP or PCI graphics card

- At least one approved hard disk (IDE or SCSI) for audio data (SCSI drives also require a SCSI card)

- SCSI card Adaptec AVA -2906

- Colour monitor with a resolution of at least 1,024 x 768 pixels

Please note that on the following systems or with the following components, problems can occur:

- Various Sony VAIO computers

- Motherboards with VIA chip sets

- Various Hewlett Packard Pavilion computers

- Computers with the following AMD processors: AMD K6, K6-2/K6-III, K7

- Computers with Cyrix processors

- Computers with Pentium I processors

System Components

The following table lists the hardware components offered by Digidesign. We also explain which components are necessary for a Pro Tools system and approximately how much you can expect to pay for it. The prices are in US dollars and were Digidesign's recommended retail prices at the time the book went to press. Some prices may have increased or been reduced since that time and special offers that may be available from time to time on hardware/ software bundles in different domestic markets have obviously not been taken into account. Once you know which items you are thinking of purchasing, it is obviously a good idea to check out the internet sites listed in the Appendix to see whether there are any special offers available on the items in question.

Pro Tools|HD

Model	Components	Description	Notes	RRP
HD1	1 PCI card, latest Pro Tools software	HD Core card	Plus at least one HD audio interface	c US $7,995
HD2	2 PCI cards, latest Pro Tools software	HD Core & HD Process card	Plus at least one HD audio interface	c US $10,495
HD3	3 PCI cards, latest Pro Tools software	HD Core & 2 HD Process cards	Plus at least one HD audio interface	c US $12,995
HD Process	PCI card	HD Process card	Additional DSP card to expand an HD system	c US $3,995
192 I/O	HD audio interface	8 x AD/DA 24-bit/192kHz, 8 x AES/EBU, TDIF, ADAT I/O, AES/EBU, S/PDIF	Maximum 50 I/O channels	c US $3,995

Practical Recording 2: Pro Tools

Model	Components	Description	Notes	RRP
192 A/D Expansion Card	Interface card	16 x A/D 24-bit/192kHz	Input extension for 192 I/O	c US $1,295
192 D/A Expansion Card	Interface card	16 x D/A 24-bit/192kHz	Output extension for 192 I/O	c US $1,195
192 Digital Expansion Card	Interface card	8 x AES/EBU, 1 x TDIF, 1 x ADAT I/O	I/O extension for 192 I/O	c US $995
192 Digital I/O	HD audio interface	16 x AES/EBU (96kHz), 8 x AES/EBU (192kHz), 2 x TDIF, 2 x ADAT I/O, 2 channel AES/EBU, S/PDIF (ADAT)	maximum 50 I/O channels	c US $2,495
96 I/O	HD audio interface	8 x AD/DA 24-bit/96kHz, ADAT I/O, AES/EBU, S/PDIF	16 I/O channels	c US $1,995
PRE	audio interface	remote controllable mic preamp	A 192 I/O or 96 I/O is needed to connect to the HD cards	c US $2,495
MIDI I/O	MIDI interface	10 MIDI inputs and outputs	Connection via USB; can be used independently of Digidesign hardware	c US $595
SYNC I/O	synchroniser	generation of LTC, VITC, MTC, Super Clock, Word Clock and AES Null Clock	Can be used independently of Digidesign hardware	c US $2,095

Note: HD cards/audio interfaces and MIX cards (see below) are not compatible. Older Digidesign audio interfaces can, however, be integrated using the Legacy peripheral port of the HD audio interface.

Pro Tools|24 MIX

Model	Components	Description	Notes	RRP
MIX	1 PCI card, Pro Tools software	MIX Core card	Plus at least one audio interface (not HD!)	c $5,995
MIXplus	2 PCI cards, Pro Tools software	MIX Core and MIX Farm card	Plus at least one audio interface (not HD!)	c $7,995
MIX3	3 PCI cards, Pro Tools software	MIX Core and 2 MIX Farm cards	plus at least one audio interface (not HD!)	c $9,995
MIX Farm	1 PCI card	MIX Farm card	additional DSP card to extend a MIX system	c $3,995
888|24 I/O	audio interface	8 x AD/DA 24-bit/48kHz, 8 x, AES/EBU I/O, S/PDIF	8 I/O channels	c $3,695
882|20 I/O	audio interface	8 x AD/DA 20-bit/48kHz, S/PDIF	8 I/O channels	c $1,245

Model	Components	Description	Notes	RRP
1622 I/O	audio interface	16 x AD 20-bit/48kHz, 2 x DA 24-bit/48kHz, S/PDIF	16 input, 2 output chnls	c $1,595
24-bit ADAT Bridge I/O	audio interface	2 x ADAT I/O 24-bit/48kHz, 2 x DA 24-bit/48kHz, AES/EBU, S/PDIF	16 I/O channels	c $1,245
USD	synchroniser	generation of LTC, VITC2, MTC, Super Clock, Word Clock and AES Null Clock	can be used independently of Digidesign hardware	c $2,095

Note: MIX and HD system cards are not compatible! Older audio interfaces can be integrated into an HD system via the Legacy peripheral port of the HD interface. MIX systems are compatible with the DSP Farm cards of Pro Tools24.

Pro Tools LE

Model	Components	Description	Notes	RRP
Digi 001	1 PCI card, 1 I/O Box, Pro Tools LE software	8 x AD/DA 24-bit/48kHz, ADAT I/O, S/PDIF	2 integrated mic preamps, integrated MIDI interface	c $1,185
Digi 002	1 hardware controller with I/O interfaces, Pro Tools LE software	8 x AD/DA 24-bit/96kHz, ADAT I/O, S/PDIF, controller	4 integrated mic preamps, integrated MIDI interface, controller unit, FireWire port	c $2,965
Mbox	1 I/O Box, Pro Tools LE software	2 x AD/DA 24-bit/48kHz, S/PDIF	USB port, 2 mic preamps, headphone output	c $590

Note: Pro Tools LE systems are not compatible with the large HD and MIX systems. All that is needed to use them is a computer of a type approved by Digidesign.

Optional Accessories

Model	Components	Description	Notes	RRP
Pro Control	hardware controller	control unit for HD and MIX systems	control via Ethernet	c $11,995
Edit Pack	hardware controller	extension for Pro Control	integrated sum meters, joysticks for surround, keyboard	c $7,495
Fader Pack	hardware controller	extension for Pro Control (max 5 items)	control via Ethernet	c $6,495
Control24	hardware controller	control unit for HD and MIX systems	control via Ethernet, 16 integrated mic preamps	c $7,995
AVoption XL	1 PCI card, 1 breakout box, software	video capture system for Pro Tools HD and MIX	editing of Avid-compatible video material	c $9,995

Note: the accessories listed are not indispensable for the use of an HD or MIX system but they do expand the system functionality.

Hardware Compatibility

Hardware System	Computer	192 I/O	192 Digital I/O	96 I/O	Pre	888I24	888	882I20	882	1622	ADAT Bridge	MIDI I/O	SYN C I/O	USD	Pro Control	Controll24	AV optionIXL
HD1	√	x	x	x	z	k	k	k	k	k	k	z	z	z	z	z	z
HD2	√	x	x	x	z	k	k	k	k	k	k	z	z	z	z	z	z
HD3	√	x	x	x	z	k	k	k	k	k	k	z	z	z	z	z	z
MIX	√				z	x	x	x	x	x	x	z	z	z	z	z	z
MIXplus	√				z	x	x	x	x	x	x	z	z	z	z	z	z
MIX³	√				z	x	x	x	x	x	x	z	z	z	z	z	z
Digi 001	√											k	k	k		k	
Digi 002	√											k	k	k			
Mbox	√											z					

Key:
n = necessary
x = necessary but an alternative position exists
z = additional option
k = compatible

System Configuration

Naturally Digidesign offers other products such as hard disks, expansion chassis and the like that can be used to extend your system. There are also products ranging from hardware controllers to audio interfaces and even studio furniture offered by third-party suppliers. Many of these can be considered luxury items; the minimum requirements are covered by the Digidesign offer: an HD- or MIX-system, for example, is supplied with a core card and an audio interface, and with these elements alone the system is functional except that you have no MIDI. A full-scale configuration, on the other hand, is rather more imposing but will leave a considerable hole in your budget. Here is one example for music production:

- HD3 system
- 4 additional HD process cards
- Expansion chassis for HD process cards
- 2 HD audio interfaces 192 I/O (fully specified)
- 4 PRE microphone preamps

- 1 MIDI I/O
- 1 SYNC I/O
- Pro Control plus 5 fader packs
- SCSI64 kit
- 4 DigiDrives

In addition, you will have to budget for a suitable computer, a high-quality monitor system (up to 7.1 configuration, a number of plug-ins plus other peripheral items such as microphones, headphone amplifiers and so on. All of this will add up to a goodly sum but at the end of it, you will have a high-end studio sufficiently well equipped for any hit production.

Second-Hand Gear

In view of the cost structure of new equipment it makes sense to scour the second hand market for Pro Tools devices. These include Digidesign hardware ranging from self-contained systems such as the Digi 001 to audio interfaces and DSP cards that you can use to

Pro Tools|HD3 – Ultimate Music (with the addition of two extra HD process cards)

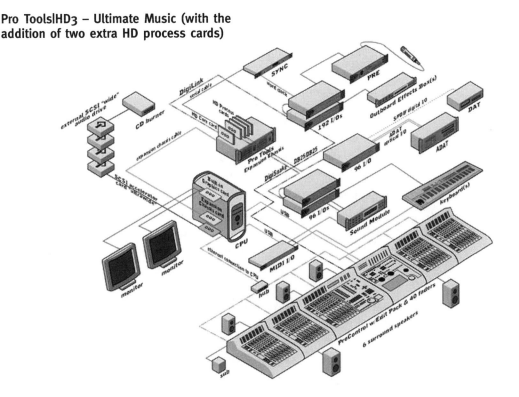

Modular, expensive and extremely powerful – this is what today's high-end studio looks like

expand your existing system or assist with the transition to Pro Tools TDM. Here there are certain aspects that need to taken into account, since the best bargain in the world will bring scant joy if the components acquired will not function together or with the system they are intended to complement.

Here are some of the most popular sources.

eBay

Probably the cheapest way of getting your hands on used Digidesign equipment is the web-based auction exchange eBay (www.ebay.com), where an unbelievable amount of professional studio equipment changes hands. Because of the enormous number and variety of goods on offer and the often vague or misleading categories into which it is divided, it can sometimes be difficult to find what you are looking for. For example, if you look in the 'Musical Instruments' section under 'Studio Equipment', you will turn up all the entries in the similarly named rubric

of the 'Audio & HiFi' section. The best method of finding Digidesign-relevant accessories is to use the Power Search function, entering search strings like 'Digidesign', 'Pro Tools', 'Protools' or 'Digi 001' and activating the option *Search titles and descriptions* to get more matches. In all probability, you will turn up all the articles currently being offered including relevant plug-ins. Naturally if you wish, you can extend the search geographically to include offers in all European countries, in the USA or world-wide. Whether or not it is worth Europeans chasing bargains in America, or vice versa, is questionable since the cost of freight is liable to take the shine off even the most attractive of bargains.

Classified Ads

Another good place to look is the Classified Advertisements section of magazines like Sound on Sound that specialise in musical instruments and recording and sound reinforcement equipment. Goods from such sources are generally offered at a fixed price – they aren't being auctioned off – but that does not mean that the seller will not listen to reasonable offers.

Refurbished Versions

Another source of used Pro Tools hardware and software is Digidesign itself. On the one hand, there are the Hardware Exchanges, these being exchange programmes run by Digidesign from the Support page of its web site. The offers change from time to time, but in October 2003, for example, four programmes were being offered:

- HD Accel Hardware Exchanges for owners of HD Process cards (in which registered owners of HD Process were invited to exchange up to HD Accel at a special price)

- Pro Tools|HD Accel Hardware Exchanges for owners of legacy TDM and Pro Tools LE-based systems

- Digi 002 and Digi 002 Rack Hardware Exchanges (in which registered owners of Digi 001, Mbox, and Digi Toolbox/Audiomedia III were invited to exchange their current systems for Digi 002 or Digi 002 Rack for a special price)

- Pro Tools|HD with AVoption|XL Hardware Exchanges (in which registered AudioVision and AVoption users were invited to move up to Pro Tools|HD with AVoption|XL for a special price)

Part-Exchange

Whichever of the part-exchange programmes is relevant to your needs, the principle is always the same: you send in your old hardware, receive a new system in return and pay the difference – you will find the exact amount displayed in the Hardware Exchange Price List. This system is convenient in that it eliminates the hassle of finding a buyer for your old hardware before embarking on the search for a replacement. You will also find on occasion that you can sell your old equipment at a considerably better price than you would have received on the open market.

User Conference

You will find another exchange for second-hand Pro Tools equipment at the Digidesign web site in what is known as the Digidesign User Conference (DUC) reached via the Support page. As well as a system-specific Questions and Answers section, there's a Buy & Sell section that registered members can use to offer used equipment for sale to an exclusive user group. There is a fair likelihood, of course, that the offer that interests you will come from the USA and that the price will be in dollars, but don't be discouraged; there's a good selection of equipment on offer and you will find you are dealing with people who know what they are talking about. Of course, transactions on the forum are entered into at your own risk. Digidesign has no involvement in the actual transaction between buyer and seller.

Music Dealers

It's also worth enquiring at your local music dealer's to see whether there are any bargains floating about. You can sometimes come across very interesting material in this way, though of course the second hand price in such cases is liable to be relatively high, since dealers naturally have to calculate rather differently than sellers on the private market.

Things To Bear In Mind
Reverse Compatibility

However attractive the prices on the second hand market may be, choosing the correct article can sometimes be tricky. Digidesign lays great emphasis – as do other manufacturers in the sector – upon the development of hardware and software that will deliver maximum performance whilst at the same time being downwards-compatible with earlier models. Occasionally, though, a point is reached where a clean break has to be made with the past to take advantage of major developments over which Digidesign has no control, such as changes in the architecture of the computer upon which the software is running. A quantum leap of this type was taken only recently with the introduction of the HD hardware, so it is safe to assume that there will not be another for at least another two years.

Take Care With Second-Hand Purchases

Users that have been working with Pro Tools for a long time and perhaps already have several generation changes behind them often find themselves asking whether or not it is worth upgrading to the latest hardware. The difficulty is that you will often find offered for sale components with names that suggest they belong to the same system, when in practice they are not even compatible. For example, anyone planning to expand their Pro Tools MIX system with a DSP Farm must make sure that the card belongs to the Pro Tools 24 hardware generation. If they should unwittingly acquire an albeit less expensive DSP Farm with Pro Tools III hardware, they will find either that they cannot use their new DSPs at all with their MIX system or else that they can only do so after an expensive chip update. The same goes for the current HD configuration, which whilst it can be combined with older interfaces, cannot be combined with MIX Farm cards, even though they may be more recent in origin than the interfaces. And even when our hypothetical Pro Tools MIX user has located the correct DSP Farm, he may well discover that the plug-ins he has purchased for his MIX system will not run on the old DSP hardware. The problem can present itself the other way round as well; Pro Tools 24 users may find they need plug-in updates before they can use their MIX Farm cards at all.

Complete Systems Are Safer

You will find yourself on far less dangerous ground if you opt for a complete system such as the Digi 001 that has undergone no changes since its introduction. With the launch of the new Digi 002 hardware, we can expect to see more Digi 001 systems turning up on the second hand market and the price should therefore drop. In the following section, we will offer some tips to help you with the choice of used Digidesign products and hopefully ensure that you end up with a stable but still economically priced system.

Checklist For Second-Hand Purchases

- Check the compatibility of the hardware; the software is naturally compatible. Ask the seller from which generation the hardware is derived and check the compatibility lists on the Digidesign home page

- The following systems/cards are definitely *not* compatible:

  - HD systems: MIX Core, MIX Farm, MIX I/O, d24, DSP Farm, Disk I/O, Digi 001, Digi 002, Project II, Session 8, Audiomedia; all NuBuss cards

  - MIX systems: DSP Farm (prior to Revision Q/Pro Tools III), Disk I/O, Digi 001, Digi 002, Project II, Session 8, Audiomedia III; all NuBuss cards

  - Digi 001 is not compatible with any other audio card

  - Digi 002 is not compatible with any other audio card

  - Mbox is not compatible with any other audio card

- HD interfaces are not compatible with older Pro Tools hardware (MIX or earlier)

- Audio interfaces such as the 442, the Session 8 Studio Interface and the Pro Master 20 are incompatible with all reasonably recent (Pro Tools 24 or later) hardware

- The 888, 882 and ADAT Bridge audio interfaces come in two versions; unlike the 888|24, 882|20 and the 24-bit ADAT Bridge, the older models work at a lower resolution

- Make sure that the audio interface is being sold with the connection cable: if you have to buy a cable of this type from Digidesign, it will set you back a fair sum

- Make sure that the seller's product registration is passed to you. Unregistered, or incorrectly registered, hardware, cannot participate in the Hardware Exchange Program

- If you acquire a plug-in with floppy disk authorisation, the seller must deliver two authorisation floppy disks for his own system (master and backup) and one for the other system (be it PC or Mac), if it is a dual-platform plug-in

- Plug-ins optimised for the DSP Farm operate uncertainly on MIX cards and will not run at all on HD systems. It may be, however, that a version of the plug-in for HD systems has been released; in the case of most plug-ins, this will turn out to be the case, and nearly all are available for registered customers free of charge upon request or else are sent to customers acquiring the HD system free of charge (iLok licence cards)

- TDM plug-ins cannot be used on Pro Tools LE systems

APPENDIX

Here we would like to offer you some interesting facts about Pro Tools, Digidesign and this book. We will begin with a short outline of the history of the company and speak to one of the company's European marketing managers. In the section 'Important Addresses', you will find the contact details of Digidesign as well as various third-party suppliers that offer plug-ins for the Pro Tools platform. There follows a list of keyboard shortcuts and a glossary designed to explain various key terms, information about the contents of the CD ROM that comes with the book and an index, to consult whenever you remember a term but have forgotten the context in which you encountered it.

Digidesign, The Company

The history of Digidesign is a typical American success story. Not perhaps success on the scale enjoyed by another US software firm – one based not a million miles from Redmond, Seattle – but success nonetheless. In the last 17 years, Digidesign has traced the trajectory of a typical successful Silicon Valley firm.

In 1985, Peter Gotcher and Evan Brooks, who played together in a band, founded Digidesign in Palo Alto; both men had an inkling of the effect the spread of computers would have on the day-to-day life of the recording studio. In the two previous years, they had also been experimenting with chips, in some cases removed from computers. Despite this experience, the two men at first concentrated their efforts upon software, which was considerably less expensive to produce, and created Pro Tools, an application that was revolutionary at the time; Digidesign's first digital recording studio allowed you to edit two audio tracks

and already featured the various edit functions still in use, though the requisite processing could take up half the day. Despite this, the new system of non tape-based recording using a computer created a sensation and the duo were encouraged to launch the first Pro Tools on the market in 1991. Version 1.0 of Pro Tools permitted the recording of four channels to hard disk and the software interface already bore the features of the system we use today.

From 1991 onwards, developments came thick and fast. with Pro Tools II, the recording capacity had increased to 16 disk and 64 virtual tracks, whilst the TDM Expansion Kit opened the door to DSP-supported audio mixing. Almost at the same time, Digidesign

Dave Lebolt, Senior Vice President of Avid Technology and General Manager of Digidesign, was formerly a professional keyboard player, producer and arranger for David Bowie, Billy Joel and Laurie Anderson, among others

introduced Session8, an economical alternative for the project studio, that could handle eight audio tracks and offered six single-band DSP filters.

Then came Pro Tools III, which in addition to cards for the connection of hard disks and the audio interface, also offered for the first time in the standard version a DSP card, the so-called DSP Farm. There followed Pro Tools 24, Pro Tools 24 MIX, MIX Plus, MIX3 and, at the beginning of 2002, Pro Tools|HD 1-3, which is currently the state of the art. With each new development, the performance of the system increased, cards were adapted to the buss interface of the host computer and the software was optimised. Anyone comparing Pro Tools|HD with its earliest ancestor, Pro Tools I, will notice similarities in the user interface, but in terms of their technical possibilities, the two systems are light years apart. And yet all this had taken only ten years.

Naturally it did not take long for these technological triumphs to be reflected in the company balance sheet. At the beginning of the '90s, Digidesign was one of the 500 fastest growing private companies in the USA, with a turnover of several million dollars. No wonder, then, that other firms began to take an interest in Digidesign. Finally, in 1995, Digidesign became part of the Avid Technology group and began to expand in new directions. AudioVision, Avid's software for the integration of image and sound data could do much, but Pro Tools combined with the AVoption proved a far more powerful vehicle for the editing of audio in conjunction with moving images.

Avid and Digidesign now dominate the entire area of image/sound production. To this date, Digidesign has sold around 150,000 systems world-wide – more than any other hardware/software solution. When today you look at the Development Partner Catalogue, in which the hardware and software products for the Pro Tools platform offered by other manufacturers are listed, you get the impression that Pro Tools has created a branch of industry all of its own, constantly nourished by the latest technological developments. All this is good news for users. Even Pro Tools Free is compatible with the state-of-the-art systems and is likely to remain so for the foreseeable future.

Digidesign And The Future

We have spoken a great deal about Pro Tools, the various systems available and the current state of the technology. What we have not yet considered is what to expect in the future. To find out, we asked Johannes Maul, Digidesign's Marketing Manager in Germany.

**Johannes Maul,
Marketing Manager of
Digidesign, Germany**

Q: Johannes, with Pro Tools|HD at the beginning of 2002, Digidesign introduced a totally new hardware platform. What new developments can we expect in the near future in the software department?

JM: With Pro Tools 6, we have introduced support for Apple's new Mac OS X, but the Windows and Macintosh platforms, however, will remain just as important to Digidesign in the future.

Q: What in your opinion could still be improved about Pro Tools, or is it perfect in your opinion?

JM: We are in close contact with the users of our systems, so we are constantly receiving feedback and important suggestions as to details that could be improved or new functions that we could introduce. The just-announced alliance with Propellerhead Software for the integration of the ReWire2 technology into Pro Tools is a good example of this. Many of our customers had approached us asking for ReWire integration and we were happy to oblige. One of the great strengths of Digidesign lies in the willingness of the most innovative minds and companies in the recording sector to work with us; indeed the number and quality of our hardware and software development partners is without equal in the industry.

Q: While Pro Tools' audio engine is constantly increasing in power and the functionality of the system in the area of audio increasing with it, the MIDI section remains bound to a specification that is now 20 years old. Is the MIDI standard really up to the demands of Pro Tools or is it time to rethink the entire approach to the control of tone generators?

JM: Using the MIDI time-stamping technology introduced with Pro Tools 6.0 for Mac OS X, it is possible to control internal tone generators with sample accuracy and the timing of external tone generators has also been improved enormously. But as well as improvements in the control of hard and software tone generators via MIDI, there are also new manipulation possibilities that would have been difficult if not impossible to realize within a classic MIDI environment; I am thinking here of the Melodyne software and Antares' Kanto synthesiser. The audio manipulation functionality will also be enhanced to make up the ground between audio and MIDI flexibility.

Q: What are Digidesign's expectations, or to put it better, what is Digidesign's vision, for the day-to-day production of the future?

JM: The market trend is towards integrated systems with the functionality of a complete studio and away from isolated individual components such as mixing consoles, effects devices, recording mediums and so on. An important factor is the scaleability of systems, in both upward and downward directions. To what extent will I be able to upgrade the capabilities of my system as expectations increase? Will it be possible to edit my sessions on a smaller system – albeit with some limitations – should that prove necessary? With Pro Tools these things are possible. The system was conceived from the start as both modular and scaleable.

Q: With the AVoption (XL) in the area of post-production, the synergy-effect of the Avid connection is apparent. Are there plans for this co-operation and functionality to extend to other systems?

JM: There is still enormous potential in the integration of the various production processes and tools. All of us in the Avid group work together intensively on all levels so as to be able to continue to offer the market the best solutions for all areas of media production – from professional high-end applications to complete solutions for use in the home.

Important Addresses

In this section you will find the most important addresses for getting in contact with Digidesign, authorised dealers and third-party suppliers. You will also find the URLs of various web sites that should prove of assistance if you encounter system problems, are planning a purchase or wish to get in contact with other Pro Tools users.

Listed first is the address of the company headquarters in Daly City, California. For the sake of completeness, you will find beneath that the address of the Customer Service Administration, which is responsible for handling product registrations, re-registrations, updates and other customer-specific services. Please note that the CSA cannot provide technical support. In Europe, you should first get in touch with your local dealer or the Digidesign branch, if there is one, in the country in which you live.

Digidesign Corporate Headquarters, USA

Digidesign, Inc
2001 Junipero Serra Blvd
Daly City, CA 94014-3886
Phone: +01-650-731-6300
Hours of business: 8:30–17:00 (Pacific Standard Time)

Customer Service

Phone: +01-650-731-6198
Fax: +01-650-731-6384 (registration by fax)
E-mail: csadmin@digidesign.com

Digidesign UK And Ireland

Digidesign Ltd
Avid Technology Europe Ltd
Pinewood Studios
Pinewood Road
Iver Heath
Bucks SL0 0NH

United Kingdom
Tel: +44 (0)1753 655 999 (9am–5:30pm)
Fax: 01753 658 600

Digidesign Technical Support

10am–5pm Mon–Fri
Warranty phone support: tel:+44 (0) 1753 653322
Non-warranty phone support: tel (premium line):
   +44 (0)906 5530919

Fax: +44 (0) 1753 658 513

Digidesign On The Internet

www.digidesign.com the most useful address if you
want to find out about products, new offers and
configurations or simply learn more about the company
and its products in general. The web site covers an
enormous range of subjects relevant to the various
Pro Tools platforms.

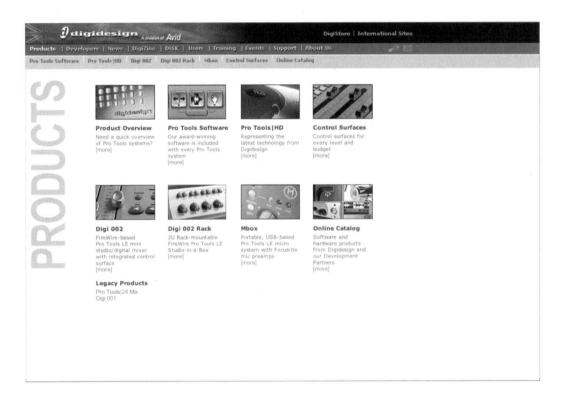

The Digidesign web site: informative and helpful

Catalogue

Here you'll find the products available for the Pro Tools
family sorted into hardware and software. In addition
to Digidesign's own products, you will find listed and
described all the offerings of third-party suppliers.

News

All the latest news is listed here. If you need to catch
up, there is also a news archive.

DigiZine

DigiZine contains info about products, application profiles
and tips from expert users. Well worth checking out.

Users

This section is a kind of Digidesign Hall of Fame in
which all the film, radio, television and (naturally) music
producers that have ever had a hit using Pro Tools are
listed and commended. And there are a goodly number!

Training

Digidesign isn't just interested in selling its products; it is also concerned to see that these products are operated by skilled personnel. This section provides information about the training programmes offered by Digidesign.

Events

What is happening elsewhere in the world? Digidesign is out and about presenting its products at trade shows, product demonstrations and the DigiWorld promotion tour. Here you can find out the venue of the next event in your neck of the woods.

Support

Here's where it gets interesting! This is where you will find the sections that well help you when you encounter problems, your configuration does not work or strange error messages start appearing on the screen. Pro Tools, whether it's TDM, LE or Free, is very stable as long as you stick to the guidelines laid down by Digidesign. You will find these guidelines set out in detail under the link Compatibility. If this fails, it sometimes helps to consult the Answer Base. Perhaps the problem has something to do with an obsolete software component; in this case, in the Download section, you may find an update that resolves it. Perhaps the information in the documentation you are using is deficient; in that case, consult the Tech Support pages to see whether a more recent edition of the manual is available that perhaps covers the point that is troubling you. A further approach is to discuss the problem with other users; perhaps one of them has encountered it and knows how it should be resolved; the Digidesign User Conference has now turned into a vast reservoir of knowledge to which users from all over the globe have contributed. And if you haven't found the answer at the end of all this, you'll just have to face up to the fact that the gods really don't like you very much!

About Digidesign

What would you like to learn about Digidesign that you do not already know? Something more about the history of the firm? The General Terms and Conditions?

Legal advice? This is the place to look. Similarly if you are looking for a dealer that sells Digidesign products in your area, wish to contact Digidesign for some other reason or would like to work for the company, these are the pages to consult.

And there's more. In the age of cyber shopping, you could hardly expect Digidesign to be trailing. The online shop in this case is called DigiStore. Although the stock is far from comprehensive, you will find plug-ins, certain hardware parts and even special offers here, as well as chic caps and shirts sporting the company logo.

DigiProNet

Digidesign's web presence, however, is more than just a place to go shopping or gather information. It offers you as a Pro Tools user an opportunity to invite the entire online community to your studio as well as a way of despatching your shoddy goods to all corners of the globe. The link DigiProNet leads to a relatively new site that is at the same time a service and a working environment. We discussed DigiStudio, the online studio option, in Chapter 10, 'Compatibility And Peripherals'. It permits you to call upon the services of other Pro Tools users to make the maximum of your session. Via DigiDelivery, you can then send the completed master to a record company, a producer or even your cousin overseas at blinding speed. You can also use this section to publicise the services you have to offer over the Internet. The AudioPages can be used for personal promotion and you can, of course, consult them, too, to see what others are getting up to. You can also purchase and download audio samples and special effects as well as entire music titles. Try persuading a sheet music dealer that you are only interested in purchasing a few bars or going into a music shop and telling them you are not interested in the entire sample CD but only one sample and that you intend to pay accordingly. And as soon as you have integrated the sample you were looking for, you can send it off to a radio station with no loss of quality or offer it for sale on an international message board.

Dealers In The UK And Ireland

For information about Pro Tools dealers across the globe, visit the Dealers section of the Digidesign website at www.digidesign.com.

Links To Third-Party Suppliers

In the following table, we've listed the most important third-party suppliers of plug-ins as well as their products. The list is sorted alphabetically and includes all the plug-in interfaces for Pro Tools. More details about individual plug-ins, manufacturers or compatibility with the variously systems/platforms can be found by following the links listed or the Software section of the Digidesign web site www.digidesign.com.

Manufacturer/Licensor	Product	Description	Link
Access	Virus TDM	software synthesiser	www.digidesign.com
	Virus Indigo	software synthesiser	
Antares	Microphone Modeler	microphone emulator	www.antarestech.com
	Auto-Tune 3	automatic intonation corrector	
Apogee	MasterTools	analyzer tool for mastering	www.apogeedigital.com
Aphex Systems	Aural Exciter	Psycho Akustik EQ emulator	www.digidesign.com
	Big Bottom Pro	Bass Enhancer emulator	
Bomb Factory	Pultec EQP-1A	Pultec EQs simulator	www.bombfactory.com
	Classic Compressors	Urei 1176 and Teletronix LA 2a compressor simulators	
	SansAmp PSA-1	guitar amp simulator	
	Voce Spin	Leslie simulator	
	Voce Chorus/Vibrato	B3 organ Leslie effects simulator	
	Moogerfooger series	simulates Bob Moog's Ring Modulator, Low-pass Filter, 12 Stage Phaser, Analog Delay	
	Joe Meek SC2/VC5	simulates Joe Meek compressors/EQs	
	BF Essentials	meter bridge, tuner, click generator, clip remover	
Dolby	Dolby Surround Tools	surround encoder/decoder	www.digidesign.com
Drawmer	Drawmer Dynamics	Drawmer compressor/gate simulator	www.digidesign.com
DUY Research	Dad Valve	valve simulation	www.duy.com
	Dad Tape	tape simulation	
	Max Duy	maximiser	
	DUY Wide	stereo image expander	
	DUY Shape	multi-band compressor	
	DUY Z-Room	reverb effect	
	DSPider	modular plug-in kit	
Focusrite	d2	high-quality EQ simulation	www.digidesign.com
	d3	high-quality compressor simulator	
IK Multimedia	AmpliTube	guitar amp simulator	www.ikmultimedia.com
Kind Of Loud	RealVerb	reverb effect, also available in a surround version	www.kindofloud.com
	Smartcode Pro	5.1 encoder	
	Tweetie/Woofie	calibration tool for speaker systems	

Manufacturer/Licensor	Product	Description	Link
Lexicon	LexiVerb	reverb effect with Lexicon quality	www.digidesign.com
Line 6	Amp Farm	guitar amp simulation	www.digidesign.com
	Echo Farm	simulator of well-known echo devices	
McDSP	Analog Channel	amplifier/tape simulator	www.mcdsp.com
	Filterbank	EQ plug-in with vintage simulators	
	Compressorbank	compressor plug-in with vintage simulators	
	MC2000	multi-band compressor	
	Synthesizer One	software synthesiser	
Metric Halo	Channelstrip	channel strip with gate, compressor, EQ, fader	www.mhlabs.com
	SpectraFoo	analyser tools	
Native Instruments	B4	B3 Hammond Organ simulator	www.native-instruments.com
	Battery	software sampler	
	NI Spektral Delay	weird delay effects	
Prosoniq	Orange Vocoder	vocoder with integrated synthesiser	www.digidesign.com
Sony	Oxford EQ	simulation of the high-end EQs of the Oxford console	www.sony.com
Synchro Arts	VocAlign	tool for lip synchronisation	www.synchroarts.co.uk
TC Works	TC Intonator	automatic intonation corrector	www.tcworks.com
	TC VoiceStrip	channel strip with gate, compressor, de-esser, EQ for vocals	
	TC Master X 3 & 5	multi-band compressor/limiter for mastering	
	TC MegaReverb	reverb effect	
	TC Chorus/Delay	TC 1210 Spatial Expander simulator	
	TC EQSAT	high-quality five-band EQ	
Wave Mechanics	Pure Pitch	pitch shifter/harmoniser	www.wavemechanics.com
	SoundBlender	weird special effects based on intonation and time correction	
	PitchDoctor	automatic intonation correction	
Waves	C4	multi-band compressor	www.waves.com
	L1/L2	maximiser	
	C1	compressor/gate	
	Q10	parametric 10-band EQ	
	S1	stereo imager	
	PS22	pseudo-stereo effect	
	SuperTap	multi-tap delay	
	MonoMod	chorus/flanger	
	Enigma	weird phase-based special effects	
	Doppler	Doppler effect	
	Meta Flanger	flanger	
	DeEsser	frequency-selective compressor	
	TrueVerb	reverb effect	

Manufacturer/Licensor	Product	Description	Link
Waves	AudioTrack	channel strip with gate, compressor and EQ	www.waves.com
	PAZ	analyser tools for mastering	
	UltraPitch	harmoniser tool	
	MaxBass	bass enhancer	
	Renaissance EQ	Six-band EQ with vintage touch	
	Renaissance Compressor	compressor with vintage touch	
	Renaissance Reverberator	simulation of vintage reverb devices	

Important Keyboard Shortcuts

If you want to work really efficiently with Pro Tools and save the maximum amount of time, you need to learn by heart the keyboard shortcuts for the most commonly used functions; it's so much faster than using the mouse. Take the time to learn them; it will save you time in the long run.

Naturally there's not enough space here to provide an exhaustive list of Pro Tools' keyboard shortcuts; there are some commands that are so esoteric that a musician will never in his entire life need to use them.

If you want to be sure of using the correct shortcut, Digidesign offers a custom keyboard in which all the shortcuts are indicated in colour on the keys. A cheaper option is the Pro Tools Label Kit – a set of scratch-proof stickers you can use to convert your existing keyboard into a custom keyboard. You do, of course, have to make sure that you are using the English (US) keyboard. If you cannot touch type and are using the French, Spanish or other keyboard, you would do better to just memorise the shortcuts you need from the following list.

For professionals – the Custom Keyboard with the shortcuts marked

Recording And Playback

Macintosh	Description	Windows
Apple-N	create new session	Ctrl-N
Apple-Shift-N	open New Track dialog	Ctrl-Shift-N
Apple-≠/Ø	cycle up/down through New Track options	Ctrl-≠/Ø
Space bar	playback start/stop	Space bar
Apple-Space bar/F12	start recording	Ctrl-Space bar/F12
Space bar	stop recording	Space bar
Apple-Full stop	stop recording and discard take	Esc or Ctrl-Full stop
Shift-Space bar	playback at half speed	Shift-Space bar
Apple-Shift-Space bar	record at half speed	Ctrl-Shift-Space bar
Apple-Shift-L	activate loop playback	Start-click on play
Option-L	activate loop record	Alt-L
Apple-Shift-P	QuickPunch	Ctrl-Shift-P
Option-K	toggle between Auto Input Monitoring and Input Only Monitoring	Alt-K

Editing

Macintosh	Description	Windows
F1	activate shuffle mode	F1
F2	activate slip mode	F2
F3	activate spot mode	F3
F4	activate grid mode	F4
F5	select Zoomer tool	F5
F6	select Trimmer tool	F6
F7	select Selector tool	F7
F8	select Grabber tool	F8
F9	select Scrubber tool	F9
F10	select Pencil tool	F10
F6 + F7 or F7 + F8	select Smart Tool	F6 + F7 or F7 + F8
Escape	cycle through edit tools	middle mouse key
~	cycle through edit modes	~
Tab	play/edit cursor to next region boundary/ sync point	Tab
Option-Tab	play/edit cursor to previous region boundary/sync point	Ctrl-Tab
Ctrl-Tab	select next region	Start-Tab
Ctrl-Option-Tab	select previous region	Start-Ctrl-Tab
Return	cursor to start of session	Enter
Option-Return	cursor to end of session	Ctrl-Enter
Enter (on keypad)	create memory location	Enter (on keypad)
Delete	delete selection in edit window	Delete

Macintosh	Description	Windows
Apple-]	horizontal zoom (larger)	Ctrl-]
Apple-[	horizontal zoom (smaller)	Ctrl-[
Apple-Option-]	vertical zoom (larger)	Ctrl-Shift-]
Apple-Option-[	vertical zoom (smaller)	Ctrl-Shift-[
Apple-C	copy selection	Ctrl-C
Apple-V	paste selection	Ctrl-V
Selection-Apple-F	open fades dialog box	Selection-Ctrl-F
Apple-Ctrl-F	use default/last selected fade shape	Ctrl-Start-F

GLOSSARY

AES/EBU
Professional-quality digital interface for the serial transfer of linearly quantized signals.

Alias File
The copy of a file that contains no data but is simply a pointer to the original and therefore consumes scarcely any storage space.

Allocator
A software utility provided with Pro Tools that allows you to see exactly how much DSP is available on your system and how it is currently being used.

Apple Talk
The network protocol used for the connection of Apple computers.

Audio Interface
A box that connects to the Digidesign audio card and offers either AD/DA converters or digital inputs and outputs or both..

AudioSuite
Non-real-time plug-in interface for native audio effects that cannot be used in the TDM mixer.

Auditioning
Monitoring an audio file using the Sound Manager prior to loading it; the Output Driver directs the signal to an audio interface.

Automation
The dynamic control of a parameter.

Auto-Punch
The automatic punching in and out at song positions determined using the Selector tool.

Auxiliary Input
A class of track that requires no voice and can be used as an effects return, for live inputs or TDM tone generators.

Backup
A safety copy of session data.

Black Burst
A clock reference signal used to synchronise audio or video devices capable of conversion to Audio Word Clock.

Bounce To Disk
A command that results in the current session (including all plug-ins) being mixed internally to disk in real-time.

Breakpoint
A step or level on a track's automation playlist..

Button
The depiction of a key on the software interface.

Channel
Any one of the physical inputs or outputs of a Pro Tools system.

Cueing
Listening to the signal during fast forward and rapid rewind.

D24 Card

An audio card without DSP power for older Pro Tools 24 systems with connectors for two audio interfaces (buss master card).

DAE Error

An error report from the Digidesign Audio Engine – consult the Digidesign Answerbase.

DAE

The Digidesign Audio Engine – the audio operating system for Digidesign hardware.

Destructive Recording

A recording that overwrites existing audio data on the hard disk.

Digi System Init

System extension that serves to initialise the Digidesign hardware.

Digi Test

A test program for Digidesign audio cards.

Direct Connect

A plug-in that allows the integration of native data streams into the TDM mixer.

Direct I/O Card

A system extension that permits the use of Digidesign hardware from within other Direct I/O compatible applications.

Disk I/O Card

An audio card for older Pro Tools systems with connections for an audio hard disk and audio interface, PCI or NuBuss (Buss Master card).

Dithering

A process whereby the quantisation noise in low resolution is overlaid with static noise spread evenly across the entire frequency spectrum.

DSP

Abbreviation of Digital Signal Processor – a chip that supplies the processing requirements of the digital mixers, plug-ins and the input and output routing.

DSP Farm

An audio card for older Pro Tools systems with 4 DSPs and an audio interface connection.

Fade

The fading in and out of audio data (using the fade function or an automated volume fade).

HD Core Card

An audio card for Pro Tools|HD systems with 9 DSPs with connections for two audio interfaces (Buss Master card); for the HD system, the TDM II mix architecture was introduced, the maximum sampling frequency being 192kHz.

HD Process Card

An audio card for Pro Tools|HD systems with nine DSPs and TDM II architecture and connections for two audio interfaces.

HTDM

Plug-in interface for tone generators that employ the host CPU.

Insertion Point

The playback cursor (equivalent to the recording/ playback head of a reel-to-reel).

Inserts

The points where plug-ins can be introduced into the signal chain of audio tracks, aux inputs and master faders.

LTC

Abbreviation of Linear Time Code – a technique used to record SMPTE time code onto magnetic tape using a dedicated time code track.

Machine Control

A software option that employs the Sony nine-pin protocol and allows you to control an external device using the Pro Tools transport controls.

MMC

Abbreviation of MIDI Machine Control – a protocol for the control of transport functions via MIDI.

MIX I/O Card

An audio card for Pro Tools MIX system without DSP power but with connectors for two audio interfaces.

MIX Core Card

Audio card for Pro Tools MIX systems with six DSPs and connectors for two audio interfaces (Buss Master card).

Mixer Plug-in

A software extension for the management of mixing and automation data as well as tracks.

MIX Farm

An audio card for Pro Tools MIX systems with 6 DSPs and connections for two audio interfaces.

MTC

Abbreviation of MIDI Time Code – SMPTE time code translated into MIDI data format.

Non-Destructive Editing

Editing that leaves the original audio material unchanged.

Nudging

The moving forwards or backwards in time of an audio or MIDI region, whereby it snaps to the nearest gridline.

OMFI

Abbreviation of Open Media Frameworks Interchange – a procedure for the encoding of image and sound files; OMFI files are designed to be read by audio and video systems regardless of platform.

OMS

Abbreviation of Open Music System – a system that handles the exchange of MIDI data between Pro Tools and other MIDI devices.

Online

In Online mode, Pro Tools can be controlled by transport commands that originate externally.

Output Driver

A driver that routes audio signals (eg system sounds) from the Sound Manager to the Digidesign hardware.

Playback Engine

The playback engine organizes the assignment of the available voices (max 96) and the DSP resources of the TDM cards.

Playlist

Playlists can contain both regions and automation data. You can create as many playlists per track as you like.

Plug-in

A software extension for the processing of audio data.

Punching In/Out

Dropping into and out of (respectively) Recording mode as a track is playing back.

Quantization

1 The forced alignment of MIDI data to a user-defined rhythmic template. 2 The process during digitisation whereby the analogue waveform is rounded to a discrete level.

QuickPunch

A recording mode that allows you to punch in and out by clicking the Record button in the Transport window.

QuickTime

Video streaming software designed by Apple.

Random Access

The ability to access data almost instantaneously from any part of a hard disk.

Region

a reference to the whole, or part, of an audio file; regions can be created by the selection of audio or MIDI data and are given names.

RTAS

Real-Time AudioSuite is a plug-in interface for host-based audio effects that can be used by the TDM mixer.

Sample Rate

The frequency at which the amplitude of an analogue audio signal is measured and digitised.

S/PDIF

Digital interface for the serial transfer of linearly quantized signals.

Scrubbing

the simulation of a tape editing technique whereby the tape is moved slowly forwards and backwards over the playback head until the desired point in the tape is found.

SCSI

Abbreviation of Small Computer System Interface – a parallel computer interface for the connection of certain hard disks, which, because of the speed at which they can store or access data, are ideally suited to the recording and playback of audio and video data.

Send

The parallel routing of the channel signal to an output or internal buss.

Session

A Pro Tools document that contains all the audio, MIDI and automation data.

Session Template

A configuration preset for Pro Tools systems.

SMPTE Time Code

A procedure for the transmission of the time position using a time code interpreted by synchronisers. SMPTE is used to synchronise tape-recorders, video machines and computer workstations.

Sound Manager

The audio operating system used by Apple Macintosh computers.

Super Clock

256x Word Clock used for the synchronisation of Digidesign's audio interfaces.

TDM

Abbreviation of time division multiplexing – interface format for plug-ins employing the DSPs of Pro Tools' hardware.

TDM Buss

An internal 24-bit buss with 256 (TDM, down to Pro tools MIX) or 512 (TDM II, from Pro Tools|HD).

Threshold

Freely selectable value relating to the amplitude/ dynamics that is used by compressors, limiters, gates and expanders.

Track Arming

The record-enabling of a track.

Track Count

The number of virtual tracks that can be played back at any one time.

Track

A virtual track in which audio or MIDI regions can be recorded, played back and edited.

Virtual Tracks

The number of tracks that can be recorded upon and cued up for playback even though they cannot be played back simultaneously. TDM systems offer 128 virtual tracks.

Voice

Like the number of voices of a synthesiser. The number of channels that can be played back simultaneously. (32 to a maximum of 96 under Pro Tools 5.3).

Volume

1 A floppy disk or hard disk drive (Mac). 2 The loudness, controlled by track faders in Pro Tools.

Word Clock

a timing signal for the synchronisation of digital audio devices or signals that is based on the sample rate. To avoid distortion, all devices linked digitally must employ the same Word Clock.